The Leo Book
Everything You Should Know About Leos

CRAFTED BY SKRIUWER

Copyright © 2025 by Skriuwer.

All rights reserved. No part of this book may be used or reproduced in any form whatsoever without written permission except in the case of brief quotations in critical articles or reviews.

At **Skriuwer**, we're more than just a team—we're a global community of people who love books. In Frisian, "Skriuwer" means "writer," and that's at the heart of what we do: creating and sharing books with readers worldwide. Wherever you are in the world, **Skriuwer** is here to inspire learning.

Frisian is one of the oldest languages in Europe, closely related to English and Dutch, and is spoken by about **500,000 people** in the province of **Friesland** (Fryslân), located in the northern Netherlands. It's the second official language of the Netherlands, but like many minority languages, Frisian faces the challenge of survival in a modern, globalized world.

We're using the money we earn to promote the Frisian language.

For more information, contact : **kontakt@skriuwer.com** (www.skriuwer.com)

TABLE OF CONTENTS

CHAPTER 1: WHAT IS LEO?

- Definition and birthdate range
- Lion symbol and traits
- Fire element and the sun's influence

CHAPTER 2: WHERE DOES LEO COME FROM?

- Ancient stargazing and early myths
- The Nemean Lion story and Hercules
- Spreading of astrological ideas

CHAPTER 3: THE MAIN TRAITS OF LEO

- Confidence and self-expression
- Warmth, kindness, and loyalty
- Creativity and leadership potential

CHAPTER 4: HOW LEO BEHAVES WITH FRIENDS

- Sharing energy and fun in groups
- Offering support and loyalty
- Possible need for balanced attention

CHAPTER 5: HOW LEO BEHAVES WITH FAMILY

- Warmth and protection at home
- Role in household organization
- Balancing personal style and family needs

CHAPTER 6: HOW LEO SHOWS FEELINGS

- Expressing emotions with honesty
- Handling ups and downs
- Combining bravery and vulnerability

CHAPTER 7: HOW LEO ACTS IN SCHOOL OR WORK

- Speaking up and taking initiative
- Leadership roles and teamwork
- Coping with rules and authority

CHAPTER 8: HOW LEO APPROACHES PROJECTS AND GOALS

- Big visions and planning steps
- Creativity in problem-solving
- Learning from setbacks

CHAPTER 9: HOW LEO DEALS WITH CHALLENGES

- Bravery vs. uncertainty
- Breaking problems into parts
- Seeking advice and staying flexible

CHAPTER 10: HOW LEO EXPRESSES CREATIVITY

- Art, performance, and inventive ideas
- Finding motivation in self-expression
- Working solo or with a team

CHAPTER 11: LEO AND PERSONAL GROWTH

- Setting goals for self-improvement
- Handling pride and listening to feedback
- Developing deeper emotional maturity

CHAPTER 12: LEO'S LIKES AND DISLIKES

- Preference for warmth and lively settings
- Drawn to creative outlets
- Taste for recognition and respect

CHAPTER 13: HOW TO GET ALONG WITH A LEO

- Showing genuine interest and honesty
- Offering support without overshadowing
- Communicating calmly during disagreements

CHAPTER 14: LEO AND COMMUNICATION

- Straightforward talking style
- Active listening and body language
- Receiving critiques thoughtfully

CHAPTER 15: LEO'S CONNECTION TO CONFIDENCE

- Self-belief vs. arrogance
- Ways to rebuild shaken self-esteem
- Encouraging others with positive energy

CHAPTER 16: LEO AND EMOTIONS

- *Joy, anger, and hidden sadness*
- *Expressing big feelings healthily*
- *Offering warmth and protection to loved ones*

CHAPTER 17: LEO IN DIFFERENT STAGES OF LIFE

- *Childhood eagerness and pride*
- *Teen exploration of identity*
- *Adult leadership and family roles*

CHAPTER 18: LEO'S HOBBIES AND SKILLS

- *Performing arts, sports, and crafts*
- *Event planning and community projects*
- *Creativity in daily life*

CHAPTER 19: COMMON MISUNDERSTANDINGS ABOUT LEO

- *Myths around arrogance and control*
- *Introverted vs. extroverted Leos*
- *Differences in leadership styles*

CHAPTER 20: INTERESTING FACTS ABOUT LEO

- *Constellation history and star names*
- *Links to ancient myths and the Sun*
- *Modern appearances in culture and media*

CHAPTER 1: WHAT IS LEO?

Leo is one of the zodiac signs that many people talk about when they look at astrology. Astrology is a way that some people try to understand personalities, relationships, and other parts of life based on the positions of the sun, moon, and stars at the time a person is born. When someone says they are a Leo, it usually means they were born between July 23 and August 22. These dates can change slightly from year to year, but they usually stay very close to that range. If a person's birthday falls in these dates, they are often said to have the Leo zodiac sign.

The word "Leo" is Latin for lion, which is why the lion is the symbol for this zodiac sign. The image of the lion is important because it helps people remember what Leo might feel like or act like. When you think of a lion, you might think of a brave and bold animal that likes to be noticed. Lions can be strong, proud, and protective. They often care for the ones they love and keep them safe. When someone says, "I am a Leo," they are saying that these lion-like qualities might show in how they act or feel. However, it doesn't mean that every Leo is exactly the same as a lion. Astrology is a broad way of thinking about personality. People can be very different from each other even if they share a zodiac sign.

In astrology, there are twelve zodiac signs, and each one is linked to dates during the year. Each sign has its own symbol, element, planet, and other traits. Leo is part of the fire signs, along with Aries and Sagittarius. Fire signs are often described as warm, bright, and sometimes quick to show strong feelings. They can be very active and can have lots of energy. In astrology, the element of fire is about passion and creativity. Because Leo is a fire sign, it is connected to these qualities too.

Besides being a fire sign, Leo is also said to be ruled by the sun. In astrology, the sun is seen as a source of light and energy. It is at the center of our solar system, and it gives warmth to our planet. Because Leo is guided by the sun, some people think Leos like to be at the center of attention or want to shine in what they do. They might feel best when they can share their ideas, feelings, or skills with other people. The sun can also represent happiness, positivity, and a clear sense of self, so many Leos might show these qualities. Again, not every Leo is the same, but these are some ideas that come from the sign's link to the sun.

Because of these qualities, many people say Leo is a sign of confidence and self-expression. Some people think Leos enjoy friendly gatherings and might like making others laugh. They could be the ones who tell jokes or stories, and they might like activities that let them show their creative ideas. Some Leos also like to be leaders, much like how a lion is sometimes called the king of the jungle. This does not mean all Leos lead the same way, but they might have a natural pull toward guiding their friends or helping others decide what to do. They might speak up in groups or offer suggestions for fun activities. They might also care strongly about fairness and be protective of their loved ones, wanting everyone to feel happy and safe.

Even though Leo is often linked to confidence and warmth, every person is different. One Leo might be loud and like to talk a lot. Another Leo might be quieter but still have a strong inner sense of dignity and self-respect. Astrology describes basic qualities, but our families, friends, interests, and experiences can shape us just as much. A person could be a Leo but have a different way of showing it. That's okay, because each person finds their own path in life.

Still, many people do enjoy using astrology for fun or personal thoughts. When someone learns they are a Leo, they might explore

Leo traits to see if those ideas match how they feel or how they behave. They might notice some things that do match, such as loving music, art, or other creative things. They might notice they like spending time with friends or making new friends. They might like telling funny stories or showing something they made, like a painting or a poem. They might also feel brave when trying new things. On the other hand, they might find some traits that do not match at all, which is normal.

Leo's symbol, the lion, can also remind people that sometimes a strong personality can be both helpful and tricky. Lions can be fierce and proud, and sometimes that can come across as bossy or stubborn. In people, this could show as being very sure of themselves, which can be good because it helps them stand up for themselves. But it might also cause them to feel upset when they don't get what they want right away. Still, learning about this side of Leo can help a Leo realize that if they become too pushy, it might be better to take a moment to listen to others. Like any quality, confidence can be helpful when balanced with kindness and respect for other people's ideas.

Some people also connect Leo to the heart. This is because the lion symbol is often linked to bravery and love. In old stories, the lion is not just strong but also loving and loyal to its pride. A pride is a family group of lions, and they stick together through good and hard times. For human Leos, it can be the same. If they find a group of friends, they might stay close and protect them. They might want to share good times and fun activities with the people they care about. They might also have a lot of warmth in their hearts, which can show up as generosity or kindness.

Another idea connected to the Leo sign is creativity. Some people think Leos are often drawn to hobbies like acting, drawing, painting, writing, dancing, or singing. This might be because they have a bright energy that makes them want to share a bit of themselves with the world. They might enjoy having an audience or at least a few people to show their work to. But creativity can appear in many ways. It could be that a Leo loves to create new recipes in the kitchen, or enjoys building and designing things. Or a Leo might like to organize events with friends, making sure everyone has fun. Each person can show their creativity in a way that feels natural to them.

One more part of the Leo nature is loyalty. Because lions stand by their pride, many Leos are seen as very loyal friends or family members. They might not forget who has helped them in the past, and they can be ready to help when someone needs them. This can be a positive quality that makes people trust them and feel safe around them. Sometimes, this loyalty can also mean a Leo might hold onto relationships or memories that are not good for them. It can be helpful for a Leo to recognize when a situation is no longer fair or healthy for them so they can step away in a peaceful way.

People who study astrology might also talk about how the sun's position in the sky influences Leos. Because the sun is bright and shines on everything equally, they might say Leos like fairness and honesty. They might be open about what they are feeling, sometimes wearing their hearts on their sleeves. At times, this honesty can be a wonderful thing because it can help people trust them. But if a Leo feels strongly about something, they might speak bluntly. If they are upset, they might show it right away. That can be surprising for friends or family who are not used to such strong feelings. So, like with all traits, it is helpful for a Leo to learn how to speak gently when needed.

Another common idea is that Leos have a playful side. Lions often play with each other, showing that they can be curious and happy at the same time. A Leo person might like games, sports, or jokes. They might be the ones who bring excitement to a group activity. If someone is feeling shy, a Leo might encourage them to step forward and join the fun. Leos can be very kind in this way. They might notice when someone is left out and try to bring them in so nobody feels lonely.

Sometimes, people mix up the idea of a Leo's confidence with being mean or self-centered. While it is true that some Leos might focus on themselves too much, not all do. Many try to use their bright energy to help others laugh or enjoy life. If a Leo does become too self-centered, they can learn to pay attention to their friends' needs. They can remember that sharing the spotlight is just as nice as being in it. Because a lion stands up for the pride, a person who is a Leo can also learn to look after other people's ideas and feelings. In this way, the traits of a Leo can help them be a protective and thoughtful friend.

In summary, Leo is a zodiac sign linked to the lion, the sun, and the fire element. People born around July 23 to August 22 often call themselves Leos if they follow astrology. They might relate to traits like confidence, warmth, bravery, loyalty, and creativity. They might enjoy having fun with friends, showing their talents, and caring for people they love. Still, not every Leo is exactly the same. Astrology is just one way to explore personality, and a person's life experience plays a huge role in who they become.

It can be fun to learn about Leo traits because it can offer a new way to think about ourselves or our friends. Some people might even guess if someone is a Leo based on how they talk or act. Others might share stories of Leos they know who always like to organize group events, put on a show, or lead a team. Whether you believe deeply in astrology or just find it interesting, Leo is a sign that is often described as sunny, friendly, and full of energy. There is also room for growth when a Leo learns to share the stage with others and remain open to new ideas.

Leos can think about their lion symbol as a reminder of both strength and kindness. A lion can roar loudly to make itself heard, but it can also live in a group and care for others. When a Leo keeps in mind the importance of balance, they can show both bravery and thoughtfulness. Many people respect that balance and see Leos as friends who will stand by them no matter what.

One more detail about the sun's link to Leo is the idea that it brings warmth. Many Leos might feel best in the summer, which is the season most connected to their sign. The longer days, bright weather, and cheerful mood of summer might fit a Leo well, since they can be energetic and social. This does not mean that all Leos dislike other seasons, but some Leos may feel a little extra excitement during those sunny days. They might also enjoy holidays, birthdays, or any chance to spend time doing fun activities with their loved ones.

Leo is also a sign that people talk about when they discuss leadership. In some stories, a lion is seen as a protector who keeps watch over others. This can be true for many Leos who like to step up and take charge. But good leadership is more than just telling people what to do. It can also mean guiding others in a fair way, being open to feedback, and sharing praise when others do a great job. A wise Leo leader is someone who does not let their pride get in the way of listening to others. They keep their sense of fun and creativity while also making sure everyone feels included. When a Leo does this well, they can inspire others to be brave and try their best.

Another topic is how Leo is often linked to the color gold or bright yellow. Since Leo is guided by the sun, some say these colors stand for warmth, energy, and happiness. You might see Leo-themed artwork that uses gold or yellow to show the bright spirit of the sign. Some Leos might like wearing clothes in these colors because they feel it shows their personality. Colors can be a fun way to express who we are, and Leos might enjoy using colors that match their inner spark.

Because many Leos like to show their creativity, some might also be drawn to music. For instance, a Leo might enjoy playing a musical instrument in front of an audience or singing songs for their friends. Others might prefer writing, painting, or drawing. Whatever they like, Leos often have a desire to share their work. This can make them happy because they like bringing smiles to people around them. However, some Leos might feel hurt if their work is ignored. Learning to handle feedback is something that many Leos have to practice. They might learn that even if not everyone loves their art right away, it is still worth doing. This skill can help them keep a positive outlook and continue being creative.

Because of their strong feelings, many Leos might also notice that they can get frustrated if things do not go as planned. For example, a Leo child might feel bad if a friend does not show up to a playdate or if they lose at a game. Because they care a lot about fun and fairness, it can be hard for them when something feels unfair. Over time, though, they can learn that life has ups and downs, and that sometimes we have to handle disappointment. Using their bright spirit, a Leo can bounce back and find new ways to have fun or solve a problem.

Leos can also have a warm heart when it comes to helping others. Imagine someone in school who sees a classmate struggling with homework. A Leo might step in and offer help. They might try to protect a friend from bullies or speak up if they see someone being treated poorly. This caring side is part of what makes a Leo special. They might be strong, but they also try to use that strength for good. On the other hand, a Leo might want to be recognized for their help. They can work on giving help just because it's kind, not because they want others to praise them. Still, it's normal for many people, not just Leos, to feel happy when others notice their kind actions.

When talking about what Leo is, we should remember that the zodiac sign is only one piece of a bigger astrological puzzle. In astrology, a person also has a moon sign, a rising sign, and other placements that might change how their Leo energy shows. But if we keep things simple, Leo is mainly about warmth, brightness, and confidence. These qualities can help a Leo face challenges and bring light to the lives of others.

It's also important to understand that not everyone believes in astrology, and that's okay too. Some people see it as a fun topic but not as a strict rule for how we must be. Others find meaning and comfort in it, using it as a tool for reflection. Either way, Leo remains an interesting sign because of its link to the lion and the sun. The idea of a playful, brave, and kind personality can be appealing. Whether or not a person believes in astrology, they might still connect with the themes that Leo stands for, such as strength, love, and a bright spirit.

So, to answer the question "What Is Leo?": Leo is a star sign that many people associate with bravery, heart, warmth, and a sunny personality. It is a fire sign, connected to the summer season and guided by the sun. The lion symbol reminds us of Leo's bold nature, but also its potential for kindness. When someone says they are a Leo, they might see bits of themselves in these ideas. They might like to lead, make people laugh, and create fun projects. They might care deeply for family and friends, offering support when needed. They might also enjoy activities that let them shine, like singing, acting, or any form of art.

CHAPTER 2: WHERE DOES LEO COME FROM?

Leo, as a zodiac sign, has a story that goes back to ancient times when people first started looking at the stars in the night sky. Long ago, before we had large cities with bright lights, people spent a lot of time studying the patterns of stars. They noticed that certain clusters of stars formed shapes that looked like animals, objects, or people. These shapes are called constellations. One of the constellations they saw resembled a lion, and they named it Leo. Over time, the lion constellation became connected to different myths and legends from various cultures. People also connected certain times of the year to this constellation.

In ancient Mesopotamia, which is an area that covered parts of modern-day Iraq, Syria, and Turkey, people were some of the first to map out the stars. They created some of the earliest forms of astrology, connecting the positions of the sun and planets to events on Earth. They looked at the sun's path through the sky, noticing that it passed in front of certain constellations during different parts of the year. They divided that path into twelve sections, each one aligned with a constellation. One of those constellations was Leo, the lion.

Later, ancient Egyptians also recognized the importance of the star patterns. They saw the sun's position and its effect on the seasons. Egypt often had strong sunlight and hot weather, especially during the time the sun seemed to be near the Leo constellation. Some people think that the sphinx, a giant statue with a lion's body and a human head, might be linked to these ideas about the lion's power and connection to the sun. The lion was a symbol of strength and royalty in many cultures, including Egypt. Kings and queens sometimes adopted the lion as a sign of their power.

After that, Greek culture had its own myths. One famous story involves the Nemean Lion, a huge and powerful lion that was said to have golden fur. This lion lived in a place called Nemea. It was part of the stories of Hercules (in Greek, Heracles). Hercules was a hero who had to complete many difficult tasks. One of these tasks was to defeat the Nemean Lion, which was incredibly strong and could not be hurt by normal weapons. Hercules had to figure out how to outsmart the lion. In some versions of the story, he trapped it in a cave, then used his great strength to defeat it. After the lion was defeated, Zeus, the king of the gods, is said to have placed the lion among the stars as the constellation Leo, to remind people of its power and importance.

This Greek myth is one of the main stories people think of when they hear about the Leo constellation. It shows a lion that was nearly impossible to beat, underlining how strong and brave it was. That image stuck in people's minds, and it paired well with the idea that people born under the sign of Leo might have a bold and strong nature. Over many centuries, as astrology spread, the symbol of Leo continued to be a lion, and the idea of a brave, proud sign stayed with it.

Astrology also continued to move from one place to another. It spread from ancient Mesopotamia to Greece, Egypt, Rome, and then to many other parts of the world. Different cultures added their own stories and details. But the lion shape in the stars stayed the same, and people kept linking the time of year around late July and most of August to the Leo constellation. This time of year also often feels warm, bright, and full of life, at least in the Northern Hemisphere.

So, people came to see Leo as a fire sign ruled by the sun, and they linked those sunny, warm qualities with the idea of a lion.

During the era of the Roman Empire, astrology took on some Latin names. That is why we have the Latin word "Leo" instead of a Greek word for the sign. The Romans also liked the lion as a symbol of power. They had big events in amphitheaters that sometimes involved lions. People were both afraid of and amazed by these animals. Because of all these stories, people grew used to seeing the lion as a fierce creature that also had a regal feeling. The empire's support of astrology also helped spread the zodiac signs further, making sure Leo stayed as one of the main signs.

As time went on, astrology became a common part of different cultures. During the Middle Ages, astrology found a home in some scientific studies, even though it was not always seen as science in the modern sense. People used it to try to predict events or understand personalities. Charts were drawn for kings and queens, showing the positions of the sun, moon, and planets. Leo was often present in these charts, and many rulers liked to see themselves as lions—strong and influential. The lion symbol has always been tied to leadership and courage, so it was easy for important figures to adopt it as their own sign.

In some areas, the constellation Leo was seen and named differently, but the lion image was very common across cultures. For example, in China, astrology worked differently, focusing on a different set of animal signs. Yet, the Western zodiac, with Leo as one of its central signs, continued to spread. Over time, this zodiac system grew popular across Europe, and later on, people carried it to the Americas and other parts of the world.

Even though the star group that forms Leo in the sky might not look exactly like a lion to everyone, ancient stargazers used their creativity to trace out the shape. The constellation has some bright stars, like Regulus (often called the heart of the lion). Regulus is a special star near what would be the front of the lion shape. Another star, Denebola, sits at the tail end of the lion. People used these bright points to outline a lion-like shape. This tradition carried on for centuries, passed down through books, star charts, and teachings.

So, when we ask, "Where does Leo come from?" we can see that it begins with the early practice of looking at the night sky and naming patterns of stars. Then, cultures like the Babylonians, Egyptians, and Greeks told stories about lions linked to those stars. Astrology turned those star patterns into symbols for different parts of the year. Because the sun appears in front of the constellation Leo around late July and most of August, that became the time for the Leo zodiac sign. The mythic lion's bravery and strength fit well with the qualities people saw in summer: warmth, energy, and boldness. Over many centuries, these ideas turned into the modern concept of Leo as we know it in astrology today.

We might also think about how the lion and the sun went together. In ancient times, the sun was extremely important for farming and daily life. When the sun was high in the sky and strong, crops grew, and people felt the heat of summer. In many places, the sun was honored as a powerful force. The lion, as a symbol of might, matched that force well. So, it made sense to connect the lion with the time of year when the sun was at its brightest or strongest. This made the Leo sign feel even more special because it was linked to life-giving warmth.

In modern times, most people do not use astrology for farming or for predicting world events in the same way ancient people might have. However, astrology is still popular, especially for personal reflection or fun discussions. We hear friends asking each other, "What's your sign?" or "Do you read your horoscope?" Leo often comes up as one of the more noticeable signs because it is linked with a lion's strong and flashy nature. People who feel strongly about astrology often enjoy reading about the old myths, like Hercules and the Nemean Lion, to get a sense of the sign's roots.

There is also a cultural side to Leo. Many artists, writers, and musicians throughout history have been drawn to the lion as a symbol. Paintings, statues, and stories about lions can be found in many places. From coats of arms used by medieval families to modern logos for sports teams, the lion is often used to show courage or pride. Because Leo is the lion sign in the zodiac, some Leos feel proud to share that symbol. They might wear jewelry with a lion design or have art in their room featuring a lion. These items remind them of the traits they enjoy, such as strength, warmth, and boldness.

In learning where Leo comes from, we also learn a bit about the practice of looking for patterns in the sky. People have always been fascinated by the stars and the mysteries of space. Before modern tools like telescopes, people learned a lot just by watching and recording what they saw night after night. They noticed that the sun, moon, and planets moved in certain patterns. They noticed that some stars stayed in place relative to each other, forming shapes. Over time, they created stories to explain these patterns. Leo was one such shape, and the lion story stuck because it appeared in many heroic tales.

Another factor is the link between Leo and ancient calendars. Long ago, people used the moon or the stars to mark time. Farmers needed to know when to plant and when to harvest. Some groups realized that when the sun rose in a certain part of the sky, it meant the start of a season. When the sun entered the lion constellation, it often meant the height of summer in many regions. This was a significant time for harvesting or preparing for the heat. In this way, the image of a lion, which can handle harsh conditions, fit well with the hottest part of the year.

It's interesting that while the zodiac started in the Northern Hemisphere, the patterns of seasons are different in the Southern Hemisphere. For example, in places like Australia or South America, July and August fall in winter, not summer. Yet, people there still use the same zodiac dates for Leo. Over time, astrology became more about personality and less about the exact season. So even though the sign of Leo is often thought of as a warm and sunny sign, someone living in a place where it's cold at that time might have a different experience of that season. Still, the stories of the lion and the ancient myths remain the same.

To sum up the history: Leo comes from an ancient constellation shaped by bright stars like Regulus and Denebola. Early star-watchers named it Leo, and civilizations like the Greeks, Babylonians, and Egyptians told legends about lions to explain or honor this shape. The Greek story of the Nemean Lion is often the most famous myth. Over time, the lion constellation was placed on the zodiac wheel. The zodiac wheel was divided into twelve signs, each connected to a segment of the sky that the sun passed through over the course of a year. Leo's period is roughly July 23 to August 22, though some sources vary on the exact dates. Because this time was hot and bright in many parts of the Northern Hemisphere, Leo became known as a sign of fire, energy, and a sunny personality. People then carried these ideas forward into modern astrology, making Leo one of the best-known zodiac signs.

Today, if you look up at the night sky during certain months, you can still try to spot the constellation Leo. It might help to use a star chart or an app on a phone or tablet to find which group of stars forms the lion shape. Regulus is the brightest star in Leo, so finding Regulus first can make it easier to see the rest of the constellation.

Of course, light pollution from cities can sometimes make it hard to see stars, but if you find a dark spot outside the city, you might have better luck. Seeing Leo with your own eyes can be a fun way to connect with the ancient roots of this sign.

By knowing where Leo comes from, we also understand why it holds such a strong place in people's imaginations. The stories of the fearless Nemean Lion, the link to the sun's power, and the warmth of summer all made Leo a sign that stands out. For thousands of years, people have passed down these ideas, telling children about the lion in the stars. Even people who do not pay much attention to astrology often know that Leo is connected to a lion and is considered a bold sign. This shows how lasting and widespread these ideas can be.

Finally, it is worth noting that while the stars stay mostly in the same patterns, the actual timing of the sun's path can shift over long periods because of something called precession. Precession is a slow wobble of Earth's axis that changes how we see the night sky over thousands of years. Because of this, some people argue that the dates of each zodiac sign do not line up with where the sun actually appears in front of the constellations in modern times. However, astrology usually keeps the traditional dates. This means that even if the sun might be in a slightly different position astronomically, we still stick to the same general calendar range for Leo. This traditional approach allows us to keep the same zodiac system that has been around for a long time, including the lion symbol and its stories.

CHAPTER 3: THE MAIN TRAITS OF LEO

When people talk about Leo, they usually mention that it is a sign linked with being bold, confident, and friendly. Even though each Leo is different in some ways, there are a few common traits that many Leos might share. These traits can affect how Leos act and how others see them. In this chapter, we will look at some of these main traits in detail. We will also think about how these traits can help Leos and in what ways they might create challenges if they are not balanced with care.

A Natural Sense of Confidence

One of the most often discussed traits of Leo is confidence. A Leo might seem sure of who they are or what they want. They might like to lead a group or stand at the front of a classroom to share an idea. This confidence might come from a strong inner feeling that they have something special to give. For example, in school, a Leo might raise their hand first to answer a question because they trust their instincts. In a group project, they might speak up about the best way to do something.

However, confidence can show itself in different ways. Not all Leos are loud or outgoing. Some may be quieter, but they still carry themselves in a way that feels secure and calm. They might not speak a lot, but when they do, it is often with a certain firmness that shows they believe in their words. Confidence, when balanced well, is a helpful quality. It can push Leos to try new things or stand up for what they believe is right.

But there is also a chance for confidence to become pushy or arrogant if a Leo is not careful. Sometimes, feeling very sure of oneself can mean a person forgets to listen to other opinions. This can lead to arguments or hurt feelings if someone thinks the Leo is ignoring their ideas. So it can be wise for Leos to remember that there is a lot of value in hearing what others have to say. By combining confidence with kindness, Leos can keep their bright spirit while respecting other points of view.

Warmth and Kindness

Another main trait linked to Leo is warmth. People might feel safe or included when they are around a Leo who is comfortable showing kindness. For example, a Leo might see someone who looks lonely at school and invite them to sit together at lunch. Or a Leo might go out of their way to share a snack or a joke to brighten another person's day. This kindness can make Leos wonderful friends and family members.

Warmth is often connected to the sun, which is said to guide Leo. Just as the sun gives light and heat, a kind Leo might share a sort of "emotional warmth." They might give compliments easily or show excitement when someone else does well. They might be the first to cheer when a friend wins a contest or finishes a tough task. This type of kindness can make people feel valued.

Sometimes, though, Leos need to be careful not to expect something in return for their kindness. It is easy to slip into thinking, "I was nice, so I should be praised." If a Leo does kind things only to get attention, others might feel used. So it helps for a Leo to give warmth freely, trusting that the good energy they send out will help others feel loved. When Leos practice genuine kindness, their natural warmth can be one of their best gifts to the world.

Creativity and Artistic Flair

Many Leos show a creative side. They might love music, painting, writing, dance, or acting. Because they often enjoy expressing themselves, creative activities can feel exciting. For instance, a Leo child might put on little performances at home, singing songs or doing short plays. A teenage Leo might try out for a drama club or make digital art. An adult Leo might design unique decorations for their house or plan fun events with special details.

This creativity is not limited to the arts. Some Leos might bring fresh ideas to projects at work or school. They could think of a new way to explain a concept in a presentation or find a clever solution to a tricky problem. Creativity means thinking of new possibilities, and Leos often have the energy and boldness to share these ideas with others. Their bright spark of imagination can get a group excited and moving forward.

However, creativity can feel blocked if a Leo becomes too worried about what others think. If they fear negative feedback, they might hold themselves back. Learning that not everyone will love their ideas can be an important lesson. Once Leos accept that it is okay to try new things, even if mistakes happen, they can continue to build on their creative talents. This can help them produce wonderful works of art, music, design, or any other creative field that catches their interest.

Leadership and Taking Charge

Leos often have a natural pull toward leadership. This might show up in small ways, such as organizing a game with friends, or in larger ways, like leading a team. Because of their confidence, Leos might step forward and say, "Let's do it this way." Some people appreciate this because it can make things simpler. If there is confusion, a Leo leader might bring the group together and set goals. People who want someone to guide them may welcome a Leo's take-charge energy.

In classrooms, a Leo might become the captain of a sports team or volunteer to be the leader of a group project. At home, a Leo might be the one who tells siblings what chores they should do, or the one who decides the best way to spend free time. This sense of leadership often goes hand in hand with other Leo traits, such as warmth and creativity. If a Leo wants to make things fun and also stay organized, their leadership can help everyone enjoy what they are doing.

On the other hand, it is crucial for a Leo leader to remember that other people also have ideas. A good leader listens to others and works as a team. If a Leo forgets this and always has to do things their own way, they might hurt people's feelings. Balancing leadership with respect for others can make a Leo even more successful. When they listen to feedback and encourage others, their leadership style can shine in a positive way.

Loyalty to Loved Ones

Many people talk about Leos as very loyal to family and friends. The lion symbol sometimes shows a group of lions, called a pride, that protects each other. Leos might act in a similar way. They could go to great lengths to defend someone they love or help a friend in need. This loyalty often means that Leos remember the people who have been there for them, and they stand by those people through good times and difficulties.

For instance, if a friend is being bullied, a Leo might speak up or try to find help. If a sibling is feeling sad, a Leo might do something kind to cheer them up. Loyalty can also show up in how Leos stay connected to old friends, even if they live far away. They might write notes, call, or visit whenever they can. This strong loyalty can make Leos treasured as friends or family members because they are often ready to give support.

Sometimes, though, loyalty can turn into stubbornness if a Leo remains loyal to someone who hurts them repeatedly. Learning when to step away from a harmful situation can be an important lesson. Loyalty is wonderful when it is shared in healthy relationships. But if someone takes advantage of a Leo's loyalty, the Leo might need to protect themselves. By being wise about who deserves their devotion, Leos can make sure their loyalty brings happiness and not pain.

Honesty and Straightforwardness

A common trait for Leos is the way they say what is on their mind without hiding too much. They may speak openly, showing their feelings clearly. This can make them seem straightforward or, at times, blunt. For example, if a Leo does not like a particular idea, they might say so right away. They might also show their excitement just as quickly, expressing joy when something good happens.

Being open can be helpful. Others do not have to guess how the Leo feels. It can build trust, since people know a Leo will say what they really think. But this honesty can sometimes come across as harsh if a Leo forgets to be gentle. A Leo might mean well but use words that sound too forceful. For example, telling a friend "You are doing it all wrong!" can be hurtful. A softer approach might be, "Let me share another idea with you."

Knowing how to balance honesty with kindness is key. Leos can learn to slow down and choose words that show respect for others' feelings. When they do, their honest nature becomes a strength that helps their relationships. People will respect the Leo for telling the truth in a helpful way.

High Energy and Enthusiasm

Leos often show a bright and enthusiastic approach to life. They might throw themselves into tasks with a lot of energy, whether that task is learning a new skill, taking part in a school activity, or playing a game with friends. This enthusiasm can make them fun to be around. They might encourage everyone to get excited, cheer others on, and bring a sense of fun to ordinary events.

Having a lot of energy can help a Leo accomplish their goals. If they decide to start a club at school, they might pour all their passion into planning meetings, talking to teachers, and making posters. If they have a creative hobby, they might spend hours practicing or perfecting their art. This energy can lead to big achievements and set an example for others who might be too shy to begin.

However, too much excitement can become a problem if a Leo does not also make time to rest. If they try to do everything at once, they might get tired or stressed. Also, if they are very excited and talk quickly, they might not notice others are tired or not in the mood. Learning to manage this high energy can help Leos stay balanced. It is good to remember that every person has their own pace. Slowing down sometimes can help a Leo notice other people's feelings and needs.

Possible Tendencies Toward Pride

Because the lion is often seen as proud, some Leos may feel a strong sense of self-esteem. This can be good, because it means they believe in themselves. But pride can also cause trouble if they always want to be the center of everything. They might expect others to admire them too much or become upset when they do not get the praise they think they deserve. In some cases, they might refuse to say "I'm sorry," even when they know they made a mistake, because they feel it is a sign of weakness.

Learning to say, "I was wrong," or "I'm sorry," does not mean a Leo has to lose their sense of self-worth. In fact, it can make their relationships stronger. If a Leo can admit mistakes, they will earn real respect from others. Balancing pride with humility can help a Leo be seen as both strong and caring. When used wisely, pride can fuel a Leo's ambition and help them stand up for themselves. When overused, it might distance them from friends.

Sense of Fun and Playfulness

Leos often have a playful side that shows up in jokes, games, or creative projects. They might enjoy making people laugh or planning fun parties or activities. They might also be quick to turn everyday moments into something amusing, like telling a silly story or drawing a funny picture.

This playfulness can make Leos popular among peers, because they bring a spark of joy. If a situation feels dull, a Leo might say, "Let's spice things up!" and suggest a new game or approach. Their creativity can shine in these moments. However, it is also important that Leos learn when to be serious. Sometimes, an event or task might require calm focus, and too much joking can distract people or come across as not respecting the situation. Knowing when to play and when to settle down is a skill that can help Leos in many parts of life.

Strong Willpower

Finally, a key trait for many Leos is willpower. This means that once they decide on a goal, they might keep going even when it is difficult. For instance, if a Leo wants to learn a new musical instrument, they might practice every day until they can play a song well. Or if they set their mind on winning a contest, they might train or study very hard. This strong will can make Leos appear unstoppable.

Willpower is generally a good thing, because it helps a Leo push through hurdles. But it can also cause stress if they never know when to take a break. If a Leo becomes too focused on one goal, they might miss out on other important things, such as spending time with friends or resting. Striking a balance between willpower and healthy breaks is necessary. Sometimes, stepping away from a problem or goal for a bit helps a person come back with fresh ideas.

Bringing It All Together

These main traits of Leo—confidence, warmth, creativity, leadership, loyalty, honesty, enthusiasm, pride, playfulness, and willpower—can shape how Leos see the world and how others see them. Of course, not every Leo shows every trait in the same way or at the same level. People are different, and personal experiences, family values, and the environments where they grow up can change how these traits show up.

Still, many Leos might find that these traits match at least part of who they are. It can be fun and helpful to recognize these qualities and think about how they work in everyday life. A Leo who knows they have a strong will might decide to aim for a big goal, like running a marathon or writing a story. A Leo who realizes they are too prideful at times might work on saying "I'm sorry" more easily. Knowing and understanding these traits can help a Leo become the best version of themselves.

It is also worth noting that every good trait can become too strong if used without care. Confidence can turn into pushiness, warmth can turn into wanting too much praise, and so on. By understanding these possible downfalls, a Leo can grow in a healthy way, staying mindful of how they affect others. When they do, they can light up a room with their kindness and excitement.

Lastly, it is important for Leos to remember that being a Leo is just one part of who they are. Each person has many layers to their personality. While astrology focuses on certain traits, real life is more complex. Still, learning about the main traits often connected to Leo can be a fun way to notice what comes naturally and where there might be room for growth.

All in all, Leo can be seen as a bright sign with qualities that help them stand out, whether at school, at work, or among friends. If Leos balance their strong traits in a caring way, they can become a source of light and strength for the people around them.

CHAPTER 4: HOW LEO BEHAVES WITH FRIENDS

Friends are an important part of life for many Leos, because Leos often love to be around people and share good times. Their warmth and boldness can make them fun friends to have. Yet, every friendship needs understanding and respect, and Leos can have certain ways of interacting with their pals that set them apart. In this chapter, we will explore how a Leo might behave with friends, looking at both the helpful and tricky parts of these friendships.

Bringing Energy and Fun to the Group

One thing that often stands out about Leos in a group of friends is their lively energy. They might be the first to suggest playing a new game or doing an activity that everyone can enjoy. If a Leo wants to spend an afternoon together, they might offer many ideas, such as going to the park, making art, or watching a movie. Because they like excitement, they might look for ways to make a simple meeting feel special.

This can be great for friends who enjoy staying active. A Leo's energy might help motivate people to leave the house, meet new people, or try different things. They can be a spark that keeps a group from feeling bored. Their creative mind might even think of games or events that others would not have considered. Friends who want to add some life to their daily routine often appreciate a Leo's enthusiasm.

However, if a friend is tired or prefers quiet time, they might find a Leo's energy too strong. A Leo might keep talking when others want a rest. In these moments, it helps if a Leo learns to notice when someone is overwhelmed and slow down a bit. Leos can still be themselves while letting friends have space. With practice, they can tell when the group is ready for action or when it might be better to do something calm, like chatting quietly or reading together.

Showing Loyalty to Friends

Leos are known for their loyalty, which often appears in friendships. If a friend is going through something tough, a Leo might stand by them, offering help or a listening ear. They might protect a friend who is being mistreated or speak up for them if they feel the friend cannot speak for themselves. This kind of loyalty can make a Leo a strong ally.

Friends may also notice that Leos remember small details about them. If a friend once said they love a certain type of candy, a Leo might bring it the next time they see them. Or if a friend is working hard on a project, a Leo might check on them to see how it is going. These thoughtful actions can show that a Leo truly values the friendship.

On the other hand, loyalty can lead a Leo to feel hurt if they think a friend did not stand up for them in return. For instance, if a Leo defends someone in a hard situation, they might expect that person to do the same when the roles are reversed. If that does not happen, the Leo might feel betrayed. It is important for Leos to remember that not everyone has the same way of showing loyalty. Some people might be quieter or might help in a more private way. Keeping an open mind can help a Leo avoid feeling let down. Still, for many Leos, loyalty is a key part of friendship, and it can keep them close to their favorite people for a long time.

Taking on the Role of Leader Among Friends

Leos often feel comfortable leading a group of friends. When it is time to plan a group project or a weekend hangout, they might jump in with suggestions. This can be very helpful if the group is not sure what to do. A Leo might say, "How about we do this?" and break the silence. They can organize tasks or assign roles, which can bring structure to the plan.

In many friendships, this works out well, especially if the friends like having a clear leader and are happy to follow along. But sometimes, friends might want to share leadership roles. If a Leo always takes control, a friend who also has good ideas might feel ignored. It can help if the Leo pauses and asks, "What do you think?" to each person in the group. That way, everyone feels heard.

Being a good leader also means being fair. If a Leo suggests a plan that mostly suits them, and never checks what others want, the group could become unhappy. For example, if a Leo always wants to play the same sport or watch the same type of show, some friends might lose interest. Learning to share leadership or step back sometimes is a good skill for Leos who want to maintain harmony with their friends. If they listen and try different ideas, everyone can have a better time.

Encouraging Friends and Giving Compliments

Another way Leos often show their friendship is by giving out compliments and encouragement. A Leo might notice a friend's new haircut, artwork, or outfit and say something nice right away. They might also cheer a friend on at a sports game or clap the loudest at a friend's performance. Because Leos can be enthusiastic, they often share that enthusiasm with the people they care about.

This can help friends feel more confident. Sometimes, people do not receive enough support in their day-to-day life. A Leo who cheers them on can boost their mood. If a friend is shy about a new hobby, a Leo might say, "You're doing so great, keep it up!" and help them feel proud. These moments can strengthen the bond between friends.

However, Leos should be careful not to give compliments only when they expect compliments in return. True kindness means giving support without expecting a prize. If a Leo feels upset because a friend did not praise them back, it can cause tension. It is normal to want appreciation, but real friendship also includes being kind just because it is nice to see a friend happy. When Leos share genuine encouragement, friendships can grow stronger on both sides.

Handling Friend Conflicts

No friendship is perfect, and disagreements can happen. Because Leos may have strong opinions, conflict might arise when others also have strong opinions. For example, if a Leo wants to do something a certain way, but a friend disagrees, sparks might fly. In these moments, a Leo might raise their voice or stand firm, which can feel intense to the friend.

Learning to solve these issues calmly is important for a Leo. They can start by listening carefully to the friend's point of view before speaking. They can ask questions like, "Why do you feel that way?" or "Can you explain more?" This shows they respect the friend's thoughts. Then, they can share their own side in a gentle tone. If both sides see that they are being heard, they can find common ground more easily.

If a Leo feels very angry, it might help to take a short break. During that time, they can breathe deeply or think about whether the disagreement is worth the stress. Many times, conflicts happen because people do not fully understand each other. Because Leos are often honest, once they calm down, they can say what they feel in a clear way. This can help the friendship move past the problem and become stronger.

Being the Center of Attention vs. Sharing the Spotlight

Leos sometimes like being in the spotlight. They might tell jokes, show off a new skill, or talk about their achievements. When friends laugh or clap, the Leo might feel excited. This can be fun for everyone when it is lighthearted. But if it happens too often, some friends might feel like they never get a turn to shine.

Imagine a group of friends taking turns telling stories. If the Leo always tells the longest story and does not let others speak, it can cause frustration. Friends might think the Leo is not interested in their stories. A good friendship goes both ways, which means allowing others to share about their lives too. If Leos notice they have been talking for a while, they can pause and say, "What do you think?" or "How about you share something that happened to you today?"

Balancing the need for attention with respect for others helps a Leo keep friendships healthy. It also shows that they value what their friends bring to the table. In return, friends are more likely to appreciate the Leo's stories and excitement, because they feel included.

Generosity with Time and Gifts

Some Leos might enjoy showing they care by giving gifts or doing favors for friends. For instance, a Leo who is good at drawing might make a special picture for a friend's birthday. Or they might offer help with homework, or volunteer to teach a skill they have learned. This generosity can make friends feel valued and special.

Because Leos are often creative, the gifts they give might feel personal or original. A friend could receive a handmade card, a small craft project, or a thoughtful letter. If a Leo sees a friend in need, they might step in to do something useful. Maybe a friend's bike is broken, and the Leo helps fix it, or maybe the friend needs someone to walk their dog while they are away. This helpfulness can form a strong bond.

However, Leos should be careful not to attach strings to their gifts. If they give something and then expect the friend to act in a certain way, that can lead to disappointment. True generosity means offering help or a gift without demanding something back. It is also wise to respect a friend's boundaries; not everyone wants or needs certain kinds of help, and pressuring them can create awkward feelings.

Standing Up for Friends in Need

When a friend faces a problem—like being teased, having a tough day, or dealing with a conflict—Leos may step in to support them. Leos do not usually hold back when they see unfairness or danger. Their courage can be a shield for those they care about. For example, if someone is making fun of a friend, a Leo might say, "That's not okay," and stand right by the friend's side.

This protective instinct can help a friend feel safer, especially if they are not comfortable speaking up on their own. It can also show others that treating the Leo's friend poorly will not be tolerated. In this way, the Leo's natural leadership and bravery become a force for good.

Still, Leos should remember not to get too aggressive in defending others. If they start yelling or insulting the other person, it can cause more trouble. Sometimes, the best approach is to remain calm, report the problem to a teacher or other helper, or move away from the harmful person. By controlling their strong feelings, Leos can make a positive difference without creating a bigger issue.

Balancing Their Own Interests with Friends' Interests

It is easy for a Leo to get caught up in their own activities or talents. They might have strong hobbies or like to talk about the things they are doing. But in a friendship, it is also important to show interest in what the other person enjoys. If a friend loves science projects, reading, or collecting stickers, a caring Leo might ask questions or try to learn a bit about it. This shows respect for the friend's world.

Because Leos are confident, they might think, "If I like this, everyone else should too!" But people have different tastes. A Leo who learns to appreciate a friend's hobbies, even if they do not share them, can strengthen the friendship. They can ask, "What do you like about it?" or "Can you teach me something?" This can lead to fun conversations and better understanding.

Sometimes, Leos might need to split time between their own activities and a friend's activities. If a friend invites them to an event that is not their usual style, a Leo might still consider going for the friend's sake. Later, the friend might return the kindness by joining a Leo's favorite activity. This back-and-forth sharing helps both sides see the value in each other's interests.

Handling Their Pride in Friendships

Leos often take pride in who they are. This pride can show up in friendships in various ways, both good and bad. For example, a Leo might be proud of a skill and want to show it off to friends. That can be entertaining, as the friends get to see them excel. It can also be inspiring, as they might think, "Wow, maybe I can do something like that too!"

However, pride can create friction if a Leo never admits when they are wrong. In a friendship, it is natural to make mistakes. Maybe a Leo said something hurtful by accident. If they refuse to say "Sorry" because of pride, the friend might feel upset. Good friendships need forgiveness, which starts with admitting mistakes. Leos can practice letting go of pride in these moments, reminding themselves that being kind is more important than being right.

Another way pride shows up is in comparing themselves to friends. If a friend does well at something that the Leo wanted to do better, the Leo might feel jealous. Remembering that each person has different strengths can help. If a friend is good at drawing, maybe the Leo is good at singing or sports. Supporting each other's talents can help both friends grow.

Building Long-Lasting Friendships

Leos who balance their traits in a caring way can form deep and long-lasting friendships. Their warmth and loyalty create a strong foundation, and their courage can help them stand by friends through hard times. Many people appreciate a Leo's fun ideas and honest advice.

Over time, a friendship with a Leo might go through different phases. When times are happy, they might celebrate each other's successes. When times are tough, the Leo might stand up for the friend or provide comfort. Through these ups and downs, Leos often stay committed, because they truly value the connection.

Keeping the Friendship Balanced

In a healthy friendship, both people give and receive. For Leos, this balance can sometimes be tricky if they love attention or always want to lead. But a kind Leo who is aware of this can make sure to ask friends questions about their day or interests. They can let friends pick activities sometimes, instead of deciding everything alone.

When Leos show that they value their friends' thoughts, the friendship becomes stronger. Friends feel respected and are more likely to admire the Leo's leadership and creativity in return. This two-way respect is what keeps a friendship solid over many years. It also helps the Leo grow as a person, because they learn new ways of thinking from their friends.

Respecting Boundaries

Some people like to share every detail of their lives, while others are more private. Leos, with their outgoing nature, might want to talk and laugh openly about many topics. A friend might not be as open or might feel shy about certain subjects. Learning to respect that friend's comfort level is key.

If a Leo pushes someone to talk about something they do not want to share, it can lead to trust issues. On the flip side, if a friend needs space, a Leo can show support by giving them room. This might mean not calling too often or not pressing the friend for answers. Over time, a Leo might find a balance between being friendly and respecting the friend's personal space. This understanding can deepen the trust within the friendship.

Being Mindful of Different Personality Types

Leos are often bold and sunny, but friends come in all personality types. A Leo might have a friend who is very introverted. That friend might prefer one-on-one conversations or quiet activities. If a Leo constantly suggests group outings or noisy games, the quieter friend might feel drained or uncomfortable.

Learning about different personalities can help a Leo adjust. For a friend who is shy, they might offer smaller get-togethers or calmer settings. If a friend likes reading, maybe a Leo can plan a reading afternoon or go to a library with them. These small efforts show that the Leo cares about the friend's preferences. In return, the friend might step out of their comfort zone sometimes to join bigger gatherings. This balance helps both friends grow closer.

Friends from Different Age Groups

Leos might find themselves making friends of different ages. Because of their confidence, they can talk to adults, younger children, or peers with ease. They might enjoy helping younger kids learn something new, or they might chat comfortably with older people about ideas. This can make them quite versatile in social situations.

With younger friends, a Leo can be a guide, teaching simple skills or sharing stories. With older friends or mentors, a Leo can learn new things and ask questions. Friendships that span different age ranges can help the Leo see life from many points of view. It can also help them practice being respectful and humble when around people with more experience.

Encouraging Group Cooperation

Leos can be good at bringing people together. If a group of friends includes people with different interests, a Leo might try to find an activity that everyone can enjoy. For instance, if some friends love art and others love sports, the Leo might suggest a friendly outdoor painting event where each person creates art in the park, and then they all play a short game together afterward.

This focus on togetherness can help a group form stronger bonds. Even if friends have disagreements, a Leo can remind them of what they share in common. They might say something like, "Hey, we all like spending time together, right? Let's find a solution!" This can reduce tension and keep the group atmosphere cheerful.

Accepting and Giving Help

Some Leos might struggle with asking for help when they need it. Because they like to appear strong, they might fear looking weak. But in a healthy friendship, help goes both ways. Just as the Leo is willing to help a friend, the friend is often glad to return the favor. If a Leo tries to do everything alone, they might feel stressed, and the friend could feel left out.

Learning to say, "I'm having a tough time, can you help?" shows trust and can deepen the friendship. It also gives the friend a chance to show their support. Most people feel valued when they can be there for someone they care about. By allowing friends to help, a Leo can build a more balanced, caring friendship.

Lasting Memories with Leo Friends

Many people remember a Leo friend long after they have parted ways. Because of the Leo's boldness, warmth, or creative ideas, the experiences they share often stand out. They might put together a fun surprise for a friend's special day or plan a themed gathering that becomes the talk of the group. Years later, friends might recall those happy times and smile.

However, the most lasting memories usually come from the genuine closeness shared. A Leo friend might offer wise advice in a tough moment or simply be a companion who listens without judgment. These deeper moments can mean even more than the lively parties or group games. Leos who can balance fun with heartfelt support often become the friends that people never forget.

Learning from Differences

Just as Leos can learn from their friends, friends can learn from Leos. A friend who is nervous about speaking up might see a Leo confidently share an opinion and think, "Maybe I can do that too." Likewise, a friend who is very calm might show a Leo how to take a step back instead of always rushing forward. Through these differences, each person grows.

Leos who want to keep strong friendships can make an effort to appreciate what each friend brings. Maybe one friend is great at solving puzzles, another is an excellent cook, and another tells the best stories. By noticing and praising these strengths, a Leo can help each friend feel special. In return, the friends often respect the Leo's leadership and creativity. This exchange of talents can make the group more fun and supportive.

The Importance of Trust in Friendships

Trust is key in any friendship. For Leos, trust might involve being open about feelings, since they usually do not hide them well. If a Leo is feeling sad or frustrated, trusting a friend means being willing to share those emotions instead of pretending everything is fine. Friends generally appreciate honesty, even if the Leo is usually the energetic one.

A Leo might also build trust by keeping a friend's secrets. If a friend shares something private, a Leo should not broadcast it to everyone. This can be challenging if the Leo likes to talk. But respecting privacy is a sign of maturity and care. When friends trust each other, they feel safe sharing deep parts of their lives, and that closeness can last for many years.

CHAPTER 5: HOW LEO BEHAVES WITH FAMILY

Families can shape who we are from an early age, and for a Leo, family life can feel especially important. Leos often have strong personalities, and their natural traits may shine brightly at home. Still, each Leo is different, so not all will show the same actions or attitudes in their family. In this chapter, we will explore how a Leo might behave around parents, siblings, and other relatives. We will look at the positive sides of these behaviors and also the parts that might need balance. By the end, you will have a deeper view of how Leos fit into family life and how they can share their warmth in caring ways.

Warmth and Cheer at Home

Leos are often known for their sunny energy, and this can show up in day-to-day family life. When they walk into a room, the mood might suddenly feel brighter. They might greet parents, siblings, or grandparents with a big smile or a cheerful hello. Some Leos make an effort to help everyone feel included at the dinner table. They may share funny stories from their day, making mealtime more lively.

This warmth can help families bond. A Leo might notice if a sibling is feeling a bit down and try to cheer them up with a joke or a silly face. They might offer to help a parent with a task, just to be kind. Families who appreciate open, happy energy often enjoy the presence of a Leo who likes bringing a bit of fun to everyday life.

However, it is good for Leos to make sure they do not need constant praise for their warmth. Sometimes, they might feel disappointed if family members are too busy or too tired to give them attention. Learning to share positive energy without always expecting a big reaction can help a Leo keep a steady glow in the home. By being patient, they can see that family members value their kindness, even if they do not always show it right away.

Taking on Tasks and Chores

Because Leos often like to feel important, some may offer to do tasks or chores around the house to show they can be responsible. A Leo child might volunteer to set the table or feed a pet. A teenage Leo might enjoy taking on a leadership role by helping younger siblings with homework or organizing a play area. An adult Leo might tackle home improvements with energy.

Stepping up to handle chores can be a great way for Leos to contribute to the family. Their natural drive might push them to do things neatly or with flair. For example, a Leo might decorate a table arrangement or organize a closet in a visually nice way. By doing so, they show creativity and lighten the load for everyone else.

At the same time, some Leos might only want the chores they find interesting, leaving the less exciting tasks for others. Or they might expect a lot of thanks for their help. In a family, everyone usually needs to pitch in, whether the task is fun or dull. Learning to do chores just because it helps the household can show a more caring, mature side of Leo. It also builds goodwill among family members, who appreciate that the Leo is part of the team.

Loyalty and Protectiveness Toward Relatives

Leos often feel strong loyalty to their family. Much like a lion guarding its group, a Leo might look out for younger siblings or stand up for a parent who faces a problem. If someone outside the family says something rude about a relative, the Leo might jump to their defense right away. This protective instinct can be reassuring, especially for family members who feel shy or worried.

Parents might notice that their Leo child is quick to defend a sibling at school if someone is unkind to them. Adult Leos might be the first to support a brother or sister going through a hard time, possibly by offering advice or stepping in to help. Grandparents might also feel the Leo's loyalty when the Leo regularly visits or calls to see how they are doing.

However, Leos have to watch out for going too far. If their protective side becomes overly intense, they might get into arguments or fights that cause more harm than good. For instance, a Leo child might yell at a teacher or another student, which could get them in trouble. A calmer approach, such as talking to a trusted adult, often works better. Leos can protect their loved ones while still keeping the peace.

Desire for Respect and Recognition in the Family

Leos often like to feel recognized for their efforts. In a family setting, this could mean hoping that parents or siblings notice their school grades, sports achievements, or completed chores. A child Leo might bring home a project from school and place it in a central spot, hoping everyone will comment on it. A teenager might ask a parent to watch them practice an instrument. An adult Leo might want relatives to see their accomplishments at work or in a hobby.

There is nothing wrong with wanting a little recognition; it can motivate Leos to keep doing their best. But at times, they might feel upset if they think they are not receiving enough praise at home. Maybe everyone is busy, or they do not realize how important that praise is to the Leo. If a Leo feels ignored, they might sulk or become frustrated.

Talking openly can help. A Leo can let family members know they appreciate supportive words or a pat on the back now and then. In return, the Leo can try to understand that families have many things to manage, and constant praise is not always possible. By meeting in the middle, both the Leo and the rest of the family can keep a healthy atmosphere.

Sharing Space with Siblings

If a Leo has siblings, there can be both good and challenging moments. Leos might take on the role of the playful older sibling, teasing younger brothers or sisters in a fun way. They might create games or lead imaginative activities. If the Leo is the youngest, they might look up to an older sibling while also trying to show they have their own strengths.

Because Leos often like to stand out, they might argue with siblings who also want attention. For example, two siblings might compete over who gets to pick the family movie or game. A Leo could become frustrated if they always lose or if they feel overshadowed by a sibling. In these moments, learning to let others have a turn is key. It can help if the family sets rules, so each child knows when it is their turn to choose or lead.

Over time, a Leo can learn to share the spotlight by focusing on the fun of being together rather than on who is in charge. This approach can create more harmony with siblings. When they do share power, Leos often find that playing or working together is more enjoyable and less stressful.

Handling Family Conflicts

In any family, disagreements happen. A Leo might clash with a parent about rules, argue with a sibling over chores, or get into a debate with a cousin. Because Leos tend to have strong opinions, these conflicts can become heated if not handled calmly. A Leo might raise their voice or insist on having the final say.

When a problem arises, it helps for a Leo to take a step back and breathe. They can practice hearing the other person's side before speaking. A parent might say, "I need you to clean your room before watching TV," and the Leo might see it as unfair. Instead of reacting with anger, the Leo can ask, "Why is this important right now?" That simple question shows respect and can lead to a clearer explanation from the parent. Then, the Leo can respond more calmly, perhaps working out a plan that meets both sides' needs.

If a disagreement is with a sibling, the same steps apply. The Leo can try to see the sibling's view, be it about splitting chores or choosing an activity. If the Leo is always in charge, the sibling might feel tired of following. If the sibling never listens, the Leo might feel ignored. Talking it out with patience often helps. By meeting halfway, a Leo can show maturity and avoid ongoing arguments.

Showing Care Through Gifts and Surprises

Some Leos love giving gifts or doing small surprises for family members. They might wrap a present for a sibling's important day or cook a meal for a parent who had a long day. A Leo could also make drawings, crafts, or write kind notes to show they care. These thoughtful gestures often bring joy and can make the home feel more loving.

While giving is kind, it is best when done without expecting something back. If a Leo buys a fancy gift and then feels sad if the sibling does not react with huge excitement, this can lead to disappointment. True kindness is about doing nice things to help someone else feel good, not to get praise. Learning this difference can make a Leo's generous heart shine in a true way.

The same applies to bigger family events: if a Leo has a role in preparing food or decorations, they might do so with creativity and style. Family members may appreciate their effort, especially if they see how much heart the Leo puts into it. Even if the thanks they receive is small, a Leo can find happiness in knowing they brightened someone's day.

Balancing Family Time with Personal Interests

Leos might have many hobbies or activities that they love, such as sports, music, art, or social clubs. They often pour lots of energy into these pursuits. Sometimes, this can mean they are away from home or busy practicing. Balancing personal interests with family time can be a challenge.

If a Leo becomes too focused on personal goals, a parent or sibling might feel neglected. They could say things like, "We never see you anymore." The Leo might not realize they have been so busy. To keep harmony, a Leo can try to set aside some regular time with family, whether it is helping with dinner or watching a show together. Even short moments can help everyone stay connected.

At the same time, family members can also support the Leo's passions. If they show interest in what the Leo is doing or attend a performance, the Leo might feel proud and encouraged. This mutual support can strengthen family bonds, helping the Leo feel both free to chase their interests and close to the people they love.

Speaking Up Honestly in the Household

Honesty is something many Leos value, and they might speak their mind openly at home. If a Leo child thinks a rule is unfair, they might say so without hesitating. If a teenage Leo wants more freedom, they might press the issue with parents and explain their reasons. This honesty can lead to clearer communication because everyone knows what the Leo is thinking.

However, it is also possible for a Leo to sound harsh or stubborn. A parent might feel attacked if a Leo says, "You never let me do anything!" in a loud tone. Talking honestly with respect is more likely to be heard. Instead, the Leo could say, "I feel like I am ready for more freedom, and here is why." This calmer approach might lead to a real discussion instead of a shouting match.

A key part of honesty at home is also listening. While Leos often share their thoughts, they should also be willing to hear parents' concerns or siblings' ideas. Open conversations work best when everyone has a chance to talk. By doing this, a Leo shows that they value not only their own view but the family's well-being too.

Leadership Roles in Family Decisions

Some Leos might step into leadership roles at home. For instance, if there is a family project—like painting a room or planning a small get-together—Leos may be the first to suggest ideas. They might naturally take charge of tasks, organizing who does what and when it needs to be done. This can be helpful, since many families appreciate someone who can keep everyone on track.

Still, it is important that a Leo respects older relatives' authority. If the parents are in charge, the Leo child should not try to overrule them. Instead, they can share their suggestions politely. For older Leos, such as grown children in the family, leading with fairness is still key. They might be full of big plans, but they should consider the needs and views of everyone else involved.

When Leos handle leadership in a thoughtful way, families can benefit from their sense of direction. They might help set clear goals or deadlines, making sure tasks get done on time. This leadership should not turn bossy, though. If a Leo starts telling others how to do things without listening to feedback, frustration can arise. Balancing confidence with respect keeps family projects smooth and fun.

Emotional Support Within the Family

Leos often have big hearts, and this can make them supportive toward relatives who are struggling. If a parent is worried about finances or health, a Leo might offer kind words or a hug. If a sibling feels sad after a bad day at school, a Leo might try to cheer them up with a board game or a funny video. Their bright spirit can help shift the mood at home.

This emotional support can become a source of strength for the family. Relatives might trust the Leo with their worries, knowing they will receive warmth in return. Over time, this can make the Leo the person everyone goes to when they need a bit of hope. Many Leos value this role, as it lets them give comfort and keep everyone feeling connected.

However, a Leo also needs to take care of their own feelings. If they are always the strong one, they might start feeling tired or stressed. It is okay for Leos to admit when they need a hug or a talk. Families work best when support goes both ways. By letting others help them too, Leos can stay balanced and continue to shine their warm light on those they love.

Encouraging Family Traditions and Togetherness

Because Leos often like shared moments, they might take part in, or even spark, family activities that bring everyone closer. For example, they might suggest a weekly movie night or a simple cooking session together. These regular activities can help relatives stay in touch and create warm memories.

If there are certain customs or habits in the family—such as a special meal once a week—Leos might enjoy adding their own ideas, like a silly game or a themed dress code. They can put their creative spin on things, making each gathering feel extra fun. This can be a good outlet for a Leo's imagination while including everyone.

One thing to watch for is whether the Leo tries to control every part of these events. If they decide everything from the menu to the seating and leave no room for others to share ideas, that can take away the fun. In a healthy family environment, everyone's input matters. So a wise Leo might ask, "What would you like to do this time?" or "Does anyone have a different idea?" This ensures that togetherness feels welcoming for everyone.

Respecting Family Boundaries and Privacy

Even though Leos like to connect and keep everyone engaged, it is important to remember that some family members need personal space. A sibling might prefer to read quietly in their room, or a parent might need some downtime after work. If the Leo constantly tries to pull them into conversation or get them to do something, it can lead to stress.

By noticing a family member's body language or mood, a Leo can learn when to give them time alone. Respecting boundaries does not mean the Leo has to change their own upbeat nature. It simply means waiting for the right moments to invite someone to join in. A well-timed, "Hey, do you feel like talking now?" can be much better than bursting in with a loud story when the other person is not ready.

Leos can also respect privacy by not pushing for secrets or personal details that someone does not want to share. If a parent or sibling is not ready to talk about a problem, the Leo can offer support but avoid prying. This shows sensitivity and allows trust to build within the family.

Handling Criticism from Parents or Relatives

Sometimes, family members might give the Leo feedback on their behavior, like telling them to be more patient or to tidy up better. Because Leos can be proud, they might feel upset or defensive when criticized. A common response could be, "But I tried my best!" or "It wasn't my fault!"

Learning to handle criticism with a calm mind can help a Leo grow. Parents often mean well, wanting to guide their child to develop good habits. If the Leo can pause and think, "Maybe they have a point," they might see that the advice can lead to improvement. This does not mean the Leo has to agree with everything. But picking out the helpful parts of the feedback can be useful.

If the criticism seems unfair, a Leo can politely explain their side. Instead of shouting, they might say, "I understand your concern, but here's what happened from my view." This approach can lead to a more open discussion. Over time, learning to take feedback can strengthen a Leo's relationship with their family and help them become more mature.

Teaching Others in the Family

A Leo who has a special skill—like playing an instrument, painting, baking, or fixing gadgets—might offer to teach relatives. This is a good way for them to share their creativity and feel useful. They might hold a short lesson for a younger sibling or show a parent a new phone trick. Because of their outgoing nature, Leos often enjoy explaining things clearly and watching others learn.

Teaching can also be a bonding activity. The Leo and their relative might laugh over mistakes or cheer when a new skill is mastered. The family member learns something helpful, and the Leo practices guiding people without being bossy. This can bring them closer.

However, a Leo teacher should be patient if the learner takes longer than expected to grasp the skill. Pushing someone too hard, or getting annoyed, can ruin the fun. Staying encouraging is key. When done well, teaching can become a memorable shared experience that helps everyone appreciate each other's strengths.

Embracing Differences Within the Family

Families can include people with many personalities. Some might be quiet, while others are chatty. Some might be more logical, while others are more emotional. A Leo who embraces these differences can learn from each relative in a unique way. For example, a quiet sibling might teach the Leo about patience, while a parent who loves reading might show them the joy of calm study.

If a Leo tries to push everyone to be more like them—louder, more energetic, or more social—it can cause friction. Embracing each person's style often leads to a more relaxed home. The Leo can still share their bright ideas, but they can also notice the value in others' calmer methods. This balance helps the family function smoothly.

Dealing with Disappointment at Home

Even with a positive attitude, Leos sometimes face disappointment. They might not get the special role they wanted in a school event, or they might have to move to a different city away from friends. In these times, a Leo might lean on their family for comfort. Parents and siblings can offer hugs, advice, or just a listening ear.

Leos might feel a strong sting when things do not go their way because of their high expectations. They want to do well and hope for recognition. When reality falls short, they can feel sad or frustrated. Family members often remind them that everyone experiences setbacks. A loving family might say things like, "You did your best, and we are proud of you," or "You can try again next time."

Learning to handle disappointment with grace at home can make Leos stronger. It teaches them that not every plan works out. By talking openly with family, Leos can find new ways to cope, bounce back, and keep their bright spirit alive.

Building Confidence Within the Home

Families play a big role in shaping a Leo's confidence. When parents or older relatives show trust in a Leo's abilities, it can boost their sense of self-worth. For instance, letting a Leo pick out a color scheme for a new room or organize a small home project can send the message, "We believe in your ideas."

Meanwhile, siblings can also play a part, whether by cheering them on or being honest critics. Constructive feedback from siblings might help Leos refine their skills. If a sibling says, "Your painting looks nice, but maybe you can add more detail here," it can improve the Leo's work. Since many Leos like to shine, they often take this feedback seriously and use it to enhance their talents.

As confidence grows in a healthy way, Leos learn they do not need praise from everyone all the time. They feel self-assured because they know their own strengths. That balanced confidence can carry into friendships, school, or work, supported by the home environment where they first learned to believe in themselves.

Creating a Harmonious Atmosphere

If a Leo has grown comfortable with who they are and learned to respect their relatives, they might serve as a unifying presence in the household. Their warm personality can make family gatherings feel inviting, and their willingness to help can reduce stress. By keeping arguments short and friendly interactions long, they help the family stay close.

A calm yet upbeat approach works best. If someone else in the family is upset, the Leo can offer support without making it all about themselves. Their natural sense of leadership can help guide the family through small chores or bigger tasks. When conflicts arise, the Leo can use their honesty and bravery to address them calmly. The result can be a more peaceful home, where everyone's voices matter.

CHAPTER 6: HOW LEO SHOWS FEELINGS

Feelings can be powerful, and Leos often have a strong emotional side. They may express happiness, anger, sadness, and excitement in big, noticeable ways. At the same time, each Leo is unique. Some may be more open about emotions, while others might show them through actions instead of words. In this chapter, we will look at common ways Leos display their feelings. We will also explore how these emotional patterns can help them connect with others, and how they can avoid common pitfalls.

A Tendency to Show Joy Boldly

When Leos are happy, it can light up a room. They might beam with a broad smile, laugh heartily at jokes, or clap their hands in excitement when something good happens. Their positive feelings are usually easy to spot. This openness can make others feel happy too, like sharing in the Leo's joy.

Because of this upbeat nature, Leos might be the ones who turn an ordinary event into something fun. They might see a small victory—like finishing a school project or cooking a tasty meal—as a reason to feel proud. Sharing this happiness can encourage friends and family to notice the good things in life. It can also inspire others to be more positive.

However, it is important for a Leo to remember that not everyone will match their level of excitement. If a friend or relative is having a tough day, they might not be ready to share in the Leo's cheer. A thoughtful Leo can notice this and choose a calmer way to interact.

That way, the friend feels understood instead of pressured to feel upbeat.

Wearers of Their Heart on Their Sleeve

Many Leos do not hide their emotions easily. If they are upset or disappointed, it often shows on their faces or in their body language. If they are thrilled, they might bounce around or speak quickly. This direct display of feelings can be refreshing, because people do not have to guess what the Leo is thinking.

Yet, it can also lead to misunderstandings if the Leo's feelings are very strong. For instance, a Leo might give a loud sigh or roll their eyes when they are bored or annoyed. Others might see this as disrespectful. Leos can work on using words to say how they feel: "I'm feeling restless," or "I'm disappointed by what happened." Clear communication often prevents confusion or hurt.

Another part of being open with emotions is learning when to keep a feeling to oneself for a short time. If it is not the right moment to share a strong reaction—like in a quiet setting or during a serious discussion—waiting until later might be wise. Over time, a Leo can fine-tune their timing so their honesty remains helpful, not disruptive.

Big Expressions of Anger or Frustration

Leos sometimes get angry in a way that can surprise others. They might raise their voices, stomp their feet, or use strong words. This can happen because they often take pride in what they do and may feel deeply offended if they think someone has disrespected them. Anger can flare up if they believe a person is acting unfairly or ignoring their input.

While anger can be a natural reaction, it is helpful for Leos to find calmer ways to express frustration. Yelling or slamming doors might scare people away rather than solve a problem. If a Leo senses anger building, they might step aside, take a few deep breaths, and ask themselves: "What am I really upset about?" Then, they can explain to the other person, "I feel hurt because..." or "I believe this is unfair because..." That clear approach can lead to better understanding.

Learning to manage anger does not mean hiding it forever. Instead, it means guiding it in a healthier way. When a Leo channels their fiery side into speaking calmly but firmly, they often find that people listen more carefully. This can help them protect their pride or their values without damaging important relationships.

Deep Caring and Compassion

Although Leos can appear strong and confident, they often have a soft spot for those who are hurting or in need. Their natural warmth can turn into real compassion when a friend or relative is sad. Leos might offer comforting words, a hug, or even practical help. Because they know how it feels to care about things deeply, they can often sense when others need emotional support.

This caring nature can show up in simple acts. For example, if a Leo notices a classmate sitting alone, they might go sit with them and spark a friendly conversation. If they see someone crying, they might offer tissues or a hand on the shoulder. These moments can bring light into another person's day.

Sometimes, Leos have to remember that not everyone is ready to open up quickly. If a person prefers to be left alone, a gentle Leo will respect that. They might say, "I'm here if you need me," and give some space. True compassion involves listening to what the other person wants, rather than pushing in with too much cheer or advice.

Self-Expression Through Creativity

Feelings can be expressed in many ways, and Leos often find creative outlets for what they feel inside. They might write poems, paint pictures, or dance with passion. By channeling emotions into art or performance, Leos can share parts of themselves that are hard to put into everyday words. For instance, a Leo who is sad might write a song to express their heartbreak, while a happy Leo might choreograph a dance that shows excitement.

Artistic expression can help Leos process strong feelings in a safe and productive way. Instead of letting emotions build up, they can pour them out onto a canvas or into a story. Others who see or hear this art might connect with the Leo's feelings, leading to supportive conversations. This can deepen bonds with friends or family.

However, if a Leo becomes frustrated that their art is not praised, they could feel discouraged. It is good to remember that art is personal, and not everyone responds in the same way. Making creative works for personal growth can be rewarding, even if only a few people truly appreciate it. The key is enjoying the process of expressing feelings rather than relying too much on external applause.

Showing Love in Grand Ways

When a Leo loves someone—be it a family member, friend, or romantic partner—they might show it in a big, memorable manner. They might give large gifts, plan big surprises, or go out of their way to do favors. This can be wonderful for the person on the receiving end, who feels cherished and seen. It can also fit a Leo's style, since many enjoy grand gestures that make an impact.

At the same time, not everyone wants or needs large displays of affection. Some people feel more touched by small, daily signs of care, like a kind note or a simple check-in. A wise Leo will learn to read each person's preferences. If someone feels shy when receiving grand gestures, a smaller token might be a better choice. The point is to show love in a way that truly resonates with the other person, not just the Leo.

This also means Leos should remember love does not always need to be loud. A quiet act of kindness, like helping clean up after dinner or listening intently when someone has a problem, can speak just as strongly. Balancing these simple acts with bigger gestures helps Leos keep their relationships harmonious and meaningful.

Handling Sadness and Disappointment

Leos might feel sadness deeply, especially if they worked very hard at something and it did not turn out well. Their disappointment can be sharp. They may spend time alone, sulking or feeling low. While it is normal to be sad sometimes, Leos benefit from finding ways to lift themselves back up. They might talk to a trusted friend, engage in a hobby, or even write down their thoughts in a private journal.

One challenge is that some Leos do not want to appear vulnerable. They might pretend everything is fine, even when they are upset inside. Over time, this can build into bigger problems, like anger outbursts or ongoing gloom. Learning to share sadness with someone supportive can help the Leo release these heavy feelings. It could be a parent, a sibling, a close friend, or even a counselor.

In time, Leos can turn disappointment into motivation. They might think, "This result hurts, but I can try again or do better next time." This hopeful approach can help them move past sadness without ignoring it. By facing the feeling, they can learn from it and come out stronger.

Pride and Vulnerability

Pride is often linked to Leo. While pride can be good in moderation—helping a Leo stand tall—it can also block them from showing true feelings. They might worry that admitting pain, fear, or embarrassment will make them look weak. So they might put on a brave face even when they need help.

Learning to say "I'm struggling" can be a big step for a proud Leo. It may feel scary at first, but many discover that honest vulnerability leads to stronger connections. Friends or family who see a Leo's softer side might feel honored that the Leo trusts them. This can turn an ordinary bond into a deeper one, based on real understanding.

Also, it is okay for Leos to make mistakes or feel uncertain. No one can be perfect all the time. A healthy sense of pride means recognizing strengths while accepting that there is always room to grow. When Leos allow themselves to be human, they often find that others love them even more, because they see the Leo's heart as well as their confidence.

Eagerness to Defend and Stand Up

If a Leo feels that someone they care about is threatened, they might show strong emotion in defense. This protective streak can be seen as loyalty, and it often appears when a friend is treated unfairly. The Leo might speak out passionately, sometimes raising their voice. This can make them seem like a fierce advocate.

While such defense can be good, Leos should watch that they do not go too far. If they become too angry or accuse others without hearing the full story, it could create unnecessary fights. It might be better to ask, "What is happening here?" or "Why are you treating my friend like that?" This more thoughtful approach can solve problems faster.

Showing feelings of concern also means checking if the friend even wants that kind of help. Sometimes, a person wants to handle their own struggles quietly. A well-meaning Leo can offer support but should respect the friend's wishes. By doing so, the Leo's protective nature stays positive and appreciated instead of overwhelming.

Interest in Group Fun and Togetherness

Many Leos enjoy group activities because they get to share their excitement with others. This can reveal their feelings of happiness and belonging. When they gather people for a board game night or a music jam session, their delight shines through. They often hope everyone has a good time and might put effort into making the environment lively.

If the group energy dips, a Leo might feel disappointed or take it personally, thinking, "I failed to keep it fun." Understanding that not every event can be perfect is a lesson for Leos. Sometimes, friends or family might just be tired. It does not reflect poorly on the Leo. Balancing the desire to bring joy with the reality that moods change can help a Leo relax and keep enjoying social times.

As with love and friendship, not everyone shows their excitement loudly. A Leo might expect people to cheer or jump around, but some folks express happiness quietly. Learning to recognize different ways of having fun can help the Leo avoid feeling hurt when others do not show the same level of outward joy.

Balanced Communication About Emotions

Because Leos can feel things so deeply, they might talk about their emotions often. This can be healthy if done in a way that also allows others to share. If a Leo only talks about themselves and never asks how others feel, conversations can become one-sided. A friend might think, "They never let me speak."

A balanced approach means a Leo can say, "I had a rough day, can I tell you about it?" and then also ask, "How was your day?" By listening to another's feelings, Leos show that they value a two-way connection. This approach builds stronger bonds and can also help the Leo learn from different viewpoints.

When a Leo listens carefully, they might discover new ideas for handling their own emotions. Maybe a friend deals with stress by drawing or practicing a relaxation exercise. The Leo might try these strategies and find they help. In this way, open communication about feelings becomes a shared experience that benefits everyone.

Confidence vs. Sensitivity

Leos can sometimes appear very sure of themselves, but inside they might be quite sensitive. If someone criticizes them or ignores their effort, they can feel hurt. This mix of outer confidence and inner softness can cause confusion for friends who think, "I thought they could handle anything."

It might help the Leo to calmly explain, "I may seem strong, but your words still affect me." By doing so, they clear up misunderstandings. Friends or relatives might be more careful in how they deliver feedback, and the Leo can learn not to hide their sensitivity. Accepting one's own tender spots is part of growing into a more balanced person.

On the other hand, sensitivity can also guide a Leo to show kindness toward others who are going through tough times. Because the Leo knows the sting of hurt feelings, they might treat people with gentleness. This can lead to deeper empathy and more caring friendships.

Finding Healthy Outlets for Emotions

A Leo's big feelings can sometimes feel like a wave that needs somewhere to go. Having a healthy outlet—like sports, art, writing, or music—can help them manage these emotions in a safe way. For instance, running or playing basketball might burn off anger or frustration. Writing in a journal might clear out worries and sadness. Painting might bring calm.

Without such outlets, Leos might become restless. They could argue with others more often or feel bored. Finding a pursuit that matches their energy level and creativity can keep them steady. It also helps them feel proud of their work, turning strong emotions into something useful or beautiful.

Friends and family can support a Leo by encouraging these outlets. They might say, "You love playing guitar—why not spend some time practicing when you feel stressed?" Simple reminders can help a Leo remember that they have choices for dealing with big feelings instead of letting them burst out unexpectedly.

Seeking Appreciation for Emotional Risks

When Leos open up about their feelings, it can feel risky. They might worry about being laughed at or not taken seriously. Because they often place value on their image, being vulnerable can be scary. If someone does not respond kindly, the Leo might retreat or become defensive.

One step toward a healthier balance is accepting that not everyone will respond perfectly. Some people might be awkward or unsure how to comfort the Leo. That does not mean the Leo was wrong to share. Over time, Leos can learn to pick the right people for emotional honesty—those who have shown understanding in the past. By doing so, they reduce the chance of a bad experience.

At the same time, if a Leo friend asks you for emotional support, responding with empathy can help them trust more. Simple words like, "I hear you" or "That sounds tough" can mean a lot. This kindness can encourage the Leo to keep sharing feelings in a positive way.

Balancing Dramatic Flair

Because Leos can be dramatic when they show feelings, they might tell stories with strong voices, big gestures, or intense words. This drama can be entertaining, but it can also be overwhelming if it happens all the time. Some people might think the Leo is overreacting to small problems.

Learning to gauge the size of the problem can help. If something minor goes wrong, a calmer reaction might be more suitable. If the Leo always reacts to everything with maximum drama, people might stop taking it seriously. Saving the big reaction for truly big events can make it more meaningful.

That said, a bit of drama now and then can liven up everyday life. A funny retelling of a small mishap can make friends or family laugh. The key is knowing the difference between playful storytelling and actual emotional strain, so the Leo's flair does not turn into constant tension.

Empathy Toward Others' Feelings

Leos might feel their own emotions strongly, but it is also important for them to learn empathy—understanding the feelings of others. If a friend is sad, a Leo could ask, "How can I help?" or "Do you want to talk about it?" Instead of assuming what the friend needs, the Leo can listen to their words and watch for cues.

When Leos practice empathy, they become better at reading moods. They notice if someone's posture is slumped or if their voice sounds shaky. This awareness can guide the Leo to offer gentle support or give space, depending on the situation. Empathy also helps the Leo build stronger bonds, because people appreciate being heard and understood.

This skill can grow over time. If a Leo has not been very empathetic in the past, they can begin by paying closer attention in conversations. Even small steps, like looking someone in the eye and asking follow-up questions, can show genuine interest in what the other person feels.

Self-Reflection and Growth

Leos, with their big emotions, can benefit from taking time to reflect. After a heated argument, they might ask themselves, "Why did I become so angry?" or "Was I really mad at the person, or was I upset about something else?" This kind of self-reflection allows them to learn from each emotional moment.

They might keep a journal where they write about daily ups and downs. Over weeks or months, patterns can emerge. A Leo might see that they tend to feel anxious before a big event or that they often snap at siblings when they are tired. Knowing these patterns is the first step to changing them. A Leo could decide to get more rest or use calm words instead of yelling.

By paying attention to how they feel and why, Leos become more in control of their emotional life. This does not mean hiding who they are—it means guiding emotions so they do not spiral or harm relationships. Self-reflection can help a Leo use their passion in ways that uplift themselves and others.

Understanding Emotional Limits

Everyone has limits on how much emotional intensity they can handle, and that includes Leos. They might assume they can take on many challenges and keep smiling. But if too many problems pile up, even a strong Leo can feel overwhelmed. Recognizing these limits is key.

Leos might set some boundaries for themselves, like choosing not to read upsetting news late at night or saying "no" to extra tasks when they already feel stressed. They can also share with friends or family when things get too heavy. This openness can prevent a meltdown later. People around them might help by offering a break or practical help.

Learning that it is okay to say, "I can't handle that right now," can save Leos from emotional exhaustion. It also gives them time to rest and recharge their bright energy. After a bit of rest, they can return to their usual lively selves.

Forgiveness and Moving Forward

When Leos have been hurt, they might hold onto the sting of that hurt for a while, especially if their pride was involved. Forgiving can be hard if they feel the other person never admitted fault. However, holding grudges can keep the Leo stuck in a cycle of anger. Learning to forgive does not mean pretending nothing happened; it means letting go of the heavy feelings for one's own peace.

Forgiveness can be a process. A Leo might need time to heal and feel ready to move forward. Talking with the person involved might help, as it can clear up misunderstandings. If direct contact is not possible, the Leo can still choose to let go of anger in their heart, knowing it will free them from lingering frustration.

Being able to move on shows emotional strength. It allows Leos to focus on the positive parts of life, rather than staying stuck in past hurts. This skill can also improve relationships, because people see that the Leo is willing to work through problems rather than hold onto them forever.

Bringing Emotional Sunshine to the World

When Leos learn to handle their emotions wisely, they can be a bright presence in any setting. Their enthusiasm, kindness, and courage can lift others' spirits. They might be the friend who says, "We can do this!" when everyone else feels unsure. They could be the family member who wraps a loved one in a big hug at just the right moment.

Over time, a Leo who has practiced healthy emotional habits becomes someone others trust. Friends might seek them out for advice or comfort, knowing the Leo's heart is genuine. Family members might rely on them to keep things light during tough days. This does not mean a Leo always has to be the strong one—just that their natural spark, guided by empathy and care, can make a difference.

In the end, how Leos show feelings is a mix of their natural flair and the lessons they learn. With self-awareness, empathy, and openness, they can let their emotions shine in ways that add warmth and happiness to the world around them. By remembering that feelings are powerful yet manageable, they can stay true to themselves while building strong and loving connections.

CHAPTER 7: HOW LEO ACTS IN SCHOOL OR WORK

Leos often bring a bold presence into any group setting, and school or work is no exception. Whether they are young students, teens in high school, or adults in the workplace, many Leos have traits that shape how they handle tasks and relate to others in these environments. In this chapter, we will explore the ways a Leo might behave in a classroom or on the job, including their approach to leadership, group work, personal motivation, and their interactions with authority figures. By understanding these patterns, Leos and those around them can create supportive spaces where everyone's strengths shine.

Confidence and Willingness to Speak Up

Leos often stand out in school or work because they feel comfortable sharing their ideas. They might be the first to raise a hand in class or volunteer an opinion during a meeting. This confidence can make them valuable contributors, since they are not shy about offering solutions or bringing up problems that need to be fixed. In a classroom, a Leo might energize a discussion by asking questions or presenting their views. In a workplace, a Leo might speak up in a team meeting to suggest a new method for handling tasks.

However, this strength can also cause issues if not balanced. Sometimes, Leos might talk over quieter classmates or coworkers without meaning to. They might assume everyone wants to hear their thoughts right away. Over time, this could frustrate others who prefer to think before speaking or who do not want so much attention on one person. A thoughtful Leo can learn to pause and give others room to speak, ensuring group discussions remain fair. By waiting a moment and asking, "Does anyone else have something to add?" they show respect for different communication styles.

Passion for Creative Assignments

Leos are often drawn to tasks that let them use their imagination. In school, they might love projects that involve art, drama, storytelling, or design. In the workplace, they might excel in roles that call for brainstorming fresh ideas or developing eye-catching presentations. This creative spark can help them produce unique work that stands out from the usual.

Because they enjoy self-expression, Leos might add personal touches to their assignments. For example, a Leo student tasked with making a poster might add bright drawings and bold lettering. A Leo employee preparing a report might include engaging visuals or well-organized graphics to make the information more interesting. This willingness to go beyond basics can catch the attention of teachers, bosses, or clients, which may lead to positive feedback.

Still, Leos should remember that not every assignment or job task allows for huge creativity. Some duties might be more routine or detail-focused. A Leo who only lights up for fun tasks might neglect the basic parts of a project. Learning that every role includes some "less exciting" work can help them remain consistent. Even in these more basic tasks, they can look for small ways to bring quality and care, showing they can handle all aspects of the job rather than just the flashy parts.

Leadership in Group Projects

Group assignments and team settings often bring out a Leo's leadership side. They may naturally step forward to organize tasks and make sure everyone stays focused. In school, this could look like a Leo student dividing the project into parts and assigning each classmate a role. In a workplace, a Leo might create a timeline for a project and coordinate efforts. Because Leos tend to be confident, many people accept them as leaders without much fuss.

However, effective leadership requires listening. If a Leo decides everything alone, teammates may feel left out or resentful. A balanced approach means the Leo leader takes in all ideas, gives credit to good suggestions, and adapts when others have better plans. When Leos practice this kind of thoughtful leadership, they can unite a team and bring out everyone's strengths. Teammates often respond well to a leader who values their input, and the Leo's natural gift for motivating others can keep the group excited about the end goal.

In some cases, Leos might clash with other team members who also want to lead. This situation might create tension if no one wants to follow another's lead. Learning the art of compromise can help. A Leo could say, "I understand your point, and I appreciate your ideas. How about we combine them with mine in this way?" By suggesting a blend of approaches, Leos show they can work with others rather than insisting on being in charge.

Enthusiasm and Energy

Whether in a classroom or an office, Leos often bring an energetic vibe. They might chat excitedly before class starts or spark friendly banter during breaks at work. This energy can lighten the mood, especially when tasks feel tiring or complex. Coworkers or classmates might see the Leo as someone who lifts everyone's spirits, helping them push through challenges.

However, not everyone matches that high level of energy. If a Leo is too chatty or excited at a time when others need quiet focus, problems can arise. For instance, a Leo student might keep whispering jokes in class while classmates are trying to work. A Leo coworker might break into loud conversation while colleagues need silence to complete a tight-deadline task. Learning to read the room is a useful skill. If people seem focused or stressed, the Leo can hold back their playful side until a better moment.

When used wisely, a Leo's enthusiasm can rally others. They might suggest a brief team stretch or a quick group discussion to refocus, helping everyone feel more awake. By channeling energy into positive actions that support the group's goals, Leos can leave a strong impression without accidentally causing distractions.

Handling Rules and Authority

In many schools and workplaces, rules and authority figures play a major role. Teachers, principals, bosses, and supervisors set guidelines that everyone is expected to follow. Leos often like to do things their own way, which can sometimes clash with strict rules. As students, some Leos might question why certain rules exist or push against limits they see as unfair. In a job, they might ask why a specific process is required if they think there is a quicker way.

This willingness to question authority can be helpful if done politely. Sometimes, rules do need updating. A Leo who respectfully asks, "Could there be a better way?" might actually inspire positive change. But if a Leo challenges authority in a rude or stubborn way, it can lead to conflict. Teachers or bosses might see it as disrespectful, especially if the Leo does not listen to the reasoning behind the rule.

Finding a balance between following guidelines and offering suggestions is key. Leos can learn to frame their questions with respect: "I see we do it like this. Have we thought about trying another approach?" This shows they care about improving the system rather than just ignoring or dismissing it. If they end up having to accept the rule as is, a wise Leo can adapt gracefully. After all, part of success in school or work is learning to work within existing structures while still shining in one's own way.

Desire for Recognition

Many Leos appreciate being noticed for their efforts. In school, a Leo might work hard on a project and then hope the teacher praises them in front of the class. In a workplace, they might be thrilled by an "Employee of the Month" award or a shout-out in a team meeting. Such recognition can motivate them to keep giving their best.

However, problems can arise if a Leo becomes too focused on praise. For instance, if a Leo does not receive the top grade or the big award, they might feel let down or resentful. They might also become jealous if someone else gets recognition they had hoped for. Understanding that not all efforts result in public praise is part of growing up. Sometimes, hard work is its own reward. Also, teachers and managers have many people to support, so they might not always highlight a Leo's achievements, even if they appreciate them privately.

Learning to take pride in personal progress, rather than always looking for outside applause, can lead to healthier self-esteem. A Leo might keep a personal record of achievements—like improved grades, new skills learned, or tasks completed well—so they can see their growth even if no one else comments on it. This inner sense of pride can make their time at school or work more fulfilling.

Cooperation and Team Spirit

Though Leos often like to lead, they can also be valuable team players if they respect each person's role. In school activities such as sports teams or group performances, a Leo might shine on the field or stage, bringing energy to the rest of the team. In the workplace, they might be the coworker who organizes birthday lunches or group meetups. These actions build camaraderie and create a friendly atmosphere.

Still, being a strong team player means knowing when to step back and support someone else's moment in the spotlight. If a classmate has a big part in a play, the Leo can cheer them on rather than trying to steal the scene. If a coworker has an innovative idea, the Leo can give them the space to present it rather than jumping in too quickly. By doing so, the Leo shows genuine support for the team as a whole.

When Leos engage in healthy teamwork, their brightness and confidence can encourage others to participate more fully. They might say, "You're great at that task—would you like to lead it?" This approach helps people see the Leo as a supportive colleague or classmate, not just someone looking to stand out.

Handling Criticism and Feedback

Everyone receives feedback at some point, whether it is a teacher's comments on a paper or a boss's thoughts on a project. Leos might find criticism challenging if it feels like a blow to their pride. They could become defensive or upset when told their work needs improvement, especially if they tried very hard. This reaction is normal but can block growth if it happens too often.

Learning to view feedback as a path to better results can help Leos thrive. Instead of seeing it as a personal attack, they might think, "This is a chance to make my work stronger." They can ask questions like, "Can you show me what part you think should change?" or "What would make this clearer?" By focusing on solutions instead of hurt feelings, Leos can improve faster and show resilience.

If the feedback seems unfair, a polite conversation might clear up misunderstandings. A Leo can calmly explain their reasoning, and the teacher or boss might realize they gave incomplete instructions. Sometimes, the feedback is accurate, and the Leo needs to adjust. Sometimes, it is a matter of miscommunication. In either case, handling the critique maturely impresses authority figures and builds respect among peers.

Balancing Social Life and Responsibility

In both school and work settings, Leos may be drawn to social interactions. They might enjoy chatting with classmates between lessons or bonding with coworkers over breaks. While this can lead to strong social connections, there is a risk of losing track of responsibilities. For example, a Leo student might spend so much time talking that they forget about homework. An employed Leo might linger in the break room too long and fall behind on tasks.

Striking a balance is important. It can help to set aside specific times for chatting or relaxing and other times for serious focus. A Leo might say, "I'll work on this assignment for an hour without distraction, and then I'll join my friends for a short break." By creating a simple plan, they can enjoy social moments while still meeting deadlines.

This balance also helps reduce stress. If a Leo leaves tasks unfinished until the last minute, they might end up rushing and feeling tense. A steady approach, with clear schedules and goals, allows them to fulfill both their work duties and their desire for connection. This method can keep them on good terms with teachers, bosses, and peers who expect consistent effort.

Assertiveness and Negotiation Skills

Leos are often assertive, meaning they stand up for themselves and speak their minds. This can be helpful in situations like asking for a raise or extra responsibilities at work, or requesting an extension on an assignment if they genuinely need more time. Because they are not shy, they can express what they need in a clear way.

Negotiation is a skill that grows more important as Leos get older. In the workplace, for example, they might negotiate pay, benefits, or project timelines. If they approach these talks with respect and a willingness to hear the other side, they can often reach beneficial agreements. If they come across as too demanding, however, managers or coworkers might resist their requests.

In school, negotiation might look like respectfully asking a teacher for clarity on an assignment or seeking alternative ways to earn extra credit. A Leo who can calmly state their reasons and propose solutions might find that teachers are open to working with them. As with authority, the key is showing respect while still voicing one's needs.

Coping with Pressure and Deadlines

School tests and work deadlines can be stressful. Leos, who like to excel, might feel extra pressure to perform well. When these deadlines approach, they might channel their energy into intense bursts of productivity, staying up late to finish projects or studying hard for exams. This rush of focus can be both exciting and draining.

Managing time effectively helps Leos avoid last-minute stress. Creating a clear plan with small steps can prevent them from feeling overwhelmed. For instance, a Leo student might break a big research project into daily tasks: day one for gathering sources, day two for outlining, and so on. A Leo employee might schedule work tasks across the week, leaving some buffer time for unexpected issues. By pacing themselves, they reduce the risk of burnout or mistakes.

Another aspect is learning to ask for help when needed. If a Leo sees they cannot meet a deadline alone, they can reach out to classmates, coworkers, or mentors. They might say, "I'm stuck on this part. Can you give me some pointers?" This approach can save time and stress, yet it requires the Leo to set aside pride and admit they need assistance. Over time, they may realize that collaboration often leads to better outcomes.

Standing Up for Others

Just as Leos may stand up for friends or family outside of school or work, they might also defend classmates, coworkers, or team members in these settings. If they see someone being treated unfairly, they might speak out. In a classroom, a Leo could challenge a bully who picks on a quieter student. In an office, they might support a colleague who is not being heard.

This protective stance can create a positive environment, as people appreciate having someone who will speak on their behalf. However, Leos need to be sure they understand the situation properly before jumping into the role of defender. Sometimes, conflicts are more complicated than they appear. Asking questions first—like, "What happened here?"—can help them avoid rushing in with incomplete facts.

When used wisely, a Leo's willingness to stand up for others can earn them respect. Classmates or colleagues might feel safer voicing concerns, knowing the Leo will back them up. This can also build friendships and improve group harmony. By balancing bravery with careful understanding, Leos make a real difference in the atmosphere around them.

Mentoring and Encouraging Peers

Leos who have mastered certain skills may enjoy sharing what they know with classmates or coworkers. They might explain a tough math concept to someone who is struggling or teach a new software trick to a colleague. Teaching and encouraging can be a natural extension of a Leo's warm and confident nature.

When done with kindness, this support helps build the Leo's reputation as a team player who lifts others. The people they assist often remember the guidance and might even return the favor later. But a Leo should ensure they are not coming across as a "know-it-all." If they help in a way that feels boastful or condescending, it can annoy the very people they intend to support.

A simple approach is to ask, "Do you need help?" or "Would you like me to show you a tip I learned?" before diving in. If the other person says "Yes," the Leo can proceed. If they say "No," the Leo can step back and respect their choice. In many cases, people appreciate a gentle offer of help more than an assumption that they need saving.

Relationship with Supervisors or Teachers

Because of their strong presence, Leos might build close relationships with teachers, bosses, or mentors. They might stand out in class or at work, which can lead to extra attention. This can be a good thing if the Leo uses that attention to learn more, ask questions, and seek growth opportunities. A teacher or boss might be happy to share insights, recommend resources, or give advanced tasks to a motivated Leo.

However, if a Leo relies too much on that attention, they might expect special treatment. They could become upset if the teacher or boss does not call on them every time or does not give them the best assignments. It is important to remember that fairness means balancing the needs of the entire group, not just one person. By showing respect for others and acknowledging that everyone deserves a chance, a Leo can keep a healthy relationship with authority figures.

When a Leo genuinely wants to learn, teachers and mentors often see them as dedicated and promising. This can open doors, like internships, references, or guidance for future goals. The key is to remain humble enough to accept feedback while still showing the eagerness that Leos naturally have.

Handling Competition

School and work can involve competition. In a classroom, students might compete for top grades or performance spots. At work, employees might vie for promotions or special projects. Leos can be quite competitive, wanting to be the best or receive the most praise. This drive can fuel hard work, but it might also create stress or rivalry.

A helpful approach is to focus on self-improvement rather than just beating others. A Leo might set personal goals, like improving their grade in math from a B to an A, or boosting their sales numbers by a certain amount at work. By measuring growth against their own past performance, they keep a healthier mindset. They can still acknowledge others' successes without feeling threatened.

If a Leo sees another person win a prize or get a promotion, it can sting at first. However, congratulating that person sincerely can build goodwill. It also shows maturity, which might be remembered the next time an opportunity arises. By channeling competition into motivation rather than envy, Leos maintain positive relationships while striving for excellence.

Growing Through Mistakes

Everyone makes mistakes, and in school or work these errors can feel especially embarrassing if a Leo was aiming for a flawless performance. They might forget a line in a presentation, miscalculate a math problem, or lose an important file at work. Because pride is part of a Leo's nature, they might feel deeply upset when these slip-ups occur.

A constructive way forward is to see mistakes as part of the learning process. Once the initial disappointment fades, they can ask themselves, "What can I learn from this?" Maybe they need better planning, more practice, or a backup system for important documents. By focusing on solutions, Leos turn an uncomfortable experience into a stepping stone.

Apologizing for mistakes can also be a sign of strength. If a Leo's error caused trouble for a teacher, a boss, or teammates, saying, "I realize I made a mistake, and I'm sorry for the inconvenience," can go a long way. Then they can outline how they will avoid the same error next time. This honest approach often gains more respect than trying to hide the mistake or blame others.

Building Long-Term Friendships or Networks

School and work are places where people spend significant time together. Over months or years, many form close bonds. Leos, with their friendly and engaging style, can build a wide circle of acquaintances or even dear friends. They might exchange study tips with classmates, join extracurricular clubs, or chat with coworkers at lunch.

These connections can prove valuable. A classmate might later become a college friend or a coworker at a future job. A coworker might eventually move to another company and recommend the Leo for a position. The relationships built through genuine care and helpfulness can last far beyond the school hallways or office walls.

However, maintaining connections requires regular communication and respect. A Leo who only interacts with people to show off achievements or gain favors might burn bridges. By staying in touch, asking about others' lives, and offering help when it is needed, Leos can form lasting networks that support their growth and success.

Stress Management

Between grades, assignments, team projects, or deadlines, school and work can bring high stress. Leos who try to handle everything perfectly might find themselves overwhelmed. They could experience insomnia, mood swings, or frustration if the pressure builds too high.

One strategy is to schedule breaks and downtime. A Leo student could set a timer so every hour of study is followed by a short rest. An employee might take a short walk after working steadily on a report. Stepping away from tasks can refresh the mind and body, preventing burnout.

Another approach is sharing concerns with a trusted mentor, friend, or counselor. Talking about stress often relieves some of the burden, and others might suggest time-saving tips or comforting advice. Physical activities—like sports, dance, or even a brisk walk—can also help reduce tension. By channeling that strong Leo energy into healthy outlets, they keep stress levels in check.

Embracing Differences in the Group

Classrooms and workplaces are full of varied personalities: introverts, extroverts, logical thinkers, creative dreamers, and more. Leos, known for their bright spirits, can play a unifying role if they learn to appreciate these differences. By noticing each person's strengths, they can create an environment where everyone feels included.

For instance, a Leo student might invite the shy classmate to join a study group, recognizing that person's quiet but detailed approach. At work, a Leo might team up with a very organized colleague who can manage schedules while the Leo handles brainstorming. This balance can lead to powerful results.

Leos benefit too, as they learn new perspectives and refine their own approach. Even if someone's style seems unusual, Leos can grow by exploring how other methods or viewpoints might solve problems. This adaptability makes them more effective collaborators and might even spark unexpected inspiration for their own tasks.

Walking the Path of Growth

In the end, school and work are big parts of life, and Leos who adapt well tend to flourish. They learn to balance confidence with humility, creativity with discipline, and leadership with teamwork. They discover that recognition feels sweeter when it comes from genuine effort and cooperation. Along the way, they become more than just high performers—they become supportive classmates, reliable colleagues, and respected contributors to their fields.

By combining their natural qualities of boldness and warmth with open-mindedness, Leos can leave a positive mark wherever they go. Classmates may remember them as lively, friendly forces who made the learning experience more engaging. Coworkers may see them as motivated and caring teammates who lifted everyone's spirit. Through this process, Leos find fulfillment in the roles they play at school and work, growing into stronger, more balanced individuals every step of the way.

CHAPTER 8: HOW LEO APPROACHES PROJECTS AND GOALS

When a Leo has a target in mind—a project to complete or a dream to reach—they often bring a mix of ambition, creativity, and determination. Because Leos can be driven by recognition and personal pride, they typically want their outcomes to be outstanding. At the same time, every goal has its obstacles, and a Leo's strengths might become stumbling blocks if not balanced. In this chapter, we will look at how Leos approach tasks, from planning and motivation to dealing with setbacks and celebrating personal victories. By understanding these elements, Leos can shape their path in a way that leads to genuine success.

Eager to Start with a Bold Vision

One hallmark of a Leo is thinking big. When they form a project idea—whether it is a personal hobby project, a school assignment, or a work endeavor—they might imagine a grand end result. For instance, a Leo who wants to write a story might picture a full novel or a script for a show. If the project is an event, they might envision a large gathering with memorable features.

This vision can spark excitement. It gives a Leo something to look forward to, a sense of possibility that draws them in. Because they are not easily intimidated by the scale of a task, they may begin with enthusiasm. They might share their grand plan with friends or teammates, hoping to get everyone on board. This kind of excitement can pull in helpers who want to be part of something special.

However, large visions can also lead to difficulty if the Leo does not break them down into smaller steps. A dream to build the best science project ever is fine, but what about the daily tasks required to get there? Without a solid plan, a Leo might feel overwhelmed once the initial excitement wears off. Learning to map out the steps and set realistic milestones can keep them moving steadily toward that bold final outcome.

Drawing Motivation from Recognition

Leos often care about how others see their achievements. They might work extra hard if they think their efforts will be praised or if the project will give them a chance to shine. This can be a great source of motivation in the early stages. Knowing they might wow friends, teachers, bosses, or even a broad audience can push them to put in those extra hours.

Yet, relying too much on outside attention can cause problems. If people around them are too busy or do not show interest, the Leo could lose the drive to finish. They might think, "Why bother if no one cares?" This can lead to unfinished tasks or giving up mid-way. A healthier approach is to combine the desire for recognition with personal passion. Even if no one is watching, the Leo can remind themselves that the process still matters. They can think, "I want to do this because it excites me and helps me learn," rather than only chasing applause.

By building an inner sense of purpose, Leos can keep going even when outside support is small. This balanced mindset also helps them bounce back quickly if the final result does not receive the reaction they expected. Instead of feeling defeated, they can see the value in the project itself.

Planning and Organizing Steps

While some Leos prefer to dive into a project right away, planning can increase the odds of success. Creating a roadmap that shows what needs to be done, when it should be done, and who might help can make the process smoother. For instance, a Leo working on a community event might list tasks like booking a venue, planning the schedule, arranging decorations, and sending invitations. Each item would have a deadline and a person in charge (even if it is just the Leo themselves).

This organized approach does not always come naturally to a sign that thrives on spontaneity. Yet, many Leos who adopt such methods find that they save time and stress. They can still inject creativity at each stage, but they know the basics are covered. If the project is large, small goals serve as stepping stones that keep the Leo motivated. Checking off one part of the plan, like finishing research or buying supplies, brings a sense of progress.

That said, it is also good for Leos to remain flexible. If a new idea or challenge appears, the plan may need adjusting. A balanced Leo acknowledges that plans are a guide, not a rigid rule. By allowing space for changes, they can adapt without losing sight of the main goal.

Leveraging Creativity

Creativity is often a Leo's strong suit. They might come up with unique concepts, color schemes, storylines, or marketing pitches that catch people's attention. This flair sets them apart when working on projects, as they can transform simple tasks into something memorable. For example, a Leo designing a product prototype might add striking visuals or user-friendly features that others did not think of.

However, it is worth noting that creativity alone cannot carry a project to completion if there is no structure. A Leo's creative ideas must be linked to actual work habits. This means setting aside time to refine ideas, test them, and gather feedback. Without these steps, even the best concept might remain half-finished or disorganized.

Leos also do well to invite input from others. A creative mind can get stuck in one vision, missing better solutions. By sharing early sketches or prototypes with trusted friends or colleagues, a Leo can gain insights that improve the final result. While they might prefer to see their big idea remain pure, collaboration can reveal small flaws or inspire improvements, making the finished product stronger overall.

Leading Project Teams

When a project involves a group, many Leos naturally step into leadership roles. Their confidence and ability to spark enthusiasm can align the team around a shared goal. They might hold team meetings, assign tasks based on each person's strengths, and create a positive atmosphere. If conflicts arise, a Leo may try to solve them quickly to keep the group on track.

At the same time, good leadership requires a willingness to listen. If a Leo ignores teammates' suggestions, they risk creating tension. Some group members might withdraw their help if they feel their voices are not valued. The best Leo leaders recognize that a team succeeds when everyone contributes and feels respected. They might ask, "What do you think?" or "How can we make this plan better?" to show genuine interest in other points of view.

In large projects, a Leo might delegate tasks so they are not overwhelmed. Delegation is a skill: it involves matching the right tasks to the right people, providing clear instructions, and then trusting those people to do their jobs. Micromanaging can harm morale. So, if the Leo leader can trust teammates to handle their parts, the group often feels more motivated and proud of their roles.

Embracing Personal Ambition

Leos are known for having big ambitions. They might aim for prestigious awards, top performance, or impressive innovations. This drive can fuel long hours of work and a willingness to face challenges. If they truly believe in the project, they might push themselves to surpass expectations.

However, ambition must be balanced with realism. If a goal is set too high without the resources or time to achieve it, a Leo might end up discouraged. It can help to break the ultimate goal into intermediate targets that feel achievable. Each success along the way boosts morale and shows that progress is real.

Additionally, ambition can be a double-edged sword if it causes a Leo to be overly competitive or dismissive of others. When aiming for a high standard, a Leo should remember that sharing credit with teammates or showing kindness to competitors does not diminish their own success. Instead, it can build respect and strong relationships, which might be helpful for future goals as well.

Overcoming Setbacks and Challenges

No matter how carefully a Leo plans, problems can pop up unexpectedly. Supplies might run out, a team member might quit, or the task might be more difficult than anticipated. Because Leos often place great pride in their projects, these setbacks can feel like personal blows. Some might react with frustration or disappointment, temporarily losing their motivation.

Yet, a Leo's natural resilience can help them bounce back. After taking a moment to acknowledge the frustration, they can shift their mindset to problem-solving: "Okay, this is tough. What are my next steps?" They might brainstorm alternatives or seek advice from a mentor. They might reorder their priorities or find creative ways to handle the shortage of materials. In this sense, a setback can even spark new ideas.

Staying calm and flexible is crucial. If a Leo becomes too stubborn about their original plan, they might miss out on creative detours that lead to success. Instead, adopting a flexible approach can turn obstacles into chances to learn and adapt.

Handling Critiques of Their Work

When a project reaches a certain milestone—like a presentation, a showcase, or a launch—it often receives feedback from teachers, bosses, clients, or an audience. Leos might feel excited to display their work, but the fear of criticism can also loom. If the feedback includes negative points, a Leo might take it to heart or see it as a personal attack.

Dealing with critiques in a healthy way means separating the work from one's worth. Even if the project did not meet someone's expectations, that does not mean the Leo is a failure. Instead, they can parse which comments are useful. For example, if a teacher suggests the argument in a paper is unclear, that is a sign to refine the writing. If a boss says the design does not match the company's style, that is guidance to adjust visually.

In some cases, feedback might be unfair or overly harsh. Even then, responding calmly can keep the Leo's reputation strong. A simple, "Thank you for your input; I'll consider what you said," can show professionalism. Later, the Leo can reflect on whether the feedback has any valid points. By handling criticism with composure, they learn how to make their projects better and grow their skills for the next challenge.

Balancing Ego and Collaboration

Leos often feel proud when they achieve something special. They might want to show it off or talk about it enthusiastically. While there is nothing wrong with taking pride in hard work, an unbalanced ego can drive away potential collaborators. If a Leo always claims credit or never admits flaws, teammates might feel unrecognized.

Collaboration thrives on shared success. A Leo who says, "This project succeeded because we all did our part," can build stronger bonds. Team members feel valued and might be willing to work together again on future goals. If the Leo tries to hog the praise, others could become less cooperative.

Also, being open about mistakes can have a positive effect. If a Leo leader or project owner says, "I made an error here, and thanks to my team for helping me fix it," it shows honesty and humility. Rather than seeing it as weakness, most people respect a person who takes responsibility. This approach encourages everyone to speak up about problems earlier, preventing bigger issues down the road.

Time Management and Avoiding Burnout

Ambitious goals require time and effort. Some Leos might push themselves too hard, staying up late night after night to polish every detail. In the short term, this can produce impressive results. Over a longer period, however, it can lead to burnout, health issues, or loss of passion for the project.

A healthier route is consistent, paced work. A Leo can set regular work hours or study periods, with breaks in between. They might also schedule fun or relaxing activities to recharge. This balanced routine keeps them from collapsing under the weight of their own high standards. If they notice signs of exhaustion—like constant tiredness or irritability—it might be time to scale back for a while.

Additionally, leaning on a support system can help. Friends, teammates, or family members can step in to share tasks or provide emotional support. By distributing the load, Leos avoid putting all the pressure on themselves. They remain more focused on creativity and quality rather than simply racing the clock.

Tracking and Measuring Progress

Because Leos often aim high, it can be helpful to track how far they have come. This tracking might be as simple as a to-do list with completed tasks marked off. Or it could be more detailed, like using a spreadsheet to note milestones, deadlines, and any changes in the plan. By reviewing this regularly, a Leo sees what remains to be done and can plan accordingly.

For larger goals, such as writing a book or preparing a major presentation, progress tracking helps the Leo spot patterns. If they notice a certain type of task always takes longer than expected, they can adjust their schedule. If they see they are ahead of schedule, they might reward themselves with a short break or additional creative experimentation. This data-driven approach supports a steady path to completion.

Celebrating progress does not have to be loud or public. A simple self-pat on the back or sharing news with a close friend can bring satisfaction. This small recognition keeps motivation alive over the long haul, preventing that feeling of running endlessly without reward.

Personal Growth Through Projects

Every goal a Leo pursues can help them grow, both in skill and character. If they pay attention, they might learn not only about the project's subject matter but also about their own strengths and weaknesses. For instance, a Leo might discover they work better in the morning, or that they need to delegate more often. They might realize they are excellent at public speaking but need to improve at detailed editing.

Reflecting on these lessons after each project can shape the next one. The Leo might decide to build a team that complements their weaknesses or find software that helps with tasks they find tedious. They could practice new skills that once caused anxiety. Over time, these small adjustments create a more rounded and effective approach to any endeavor.

Personal growth also involves emotional maturity. A Leo who starts out taking every setback personally might, through repeated experiences, learn to stay calm and focused under stress. They might see that growth is ongoing and that no single project defines their entire worth. This perspective can free them to experiment more and worry less about making a perfect first impression.

Handling Multiple Goals at Once

Sometimes, a Leo might juggle several projects or ambitions simultaneously. Maybe they are pursuing a main career goal, developing a side hobby, and also planning a personal event. Their enthusiasm can push them to say "Yes" to many opportunities. While this can be thrilling, it can also strain their energy.

Successful multi-goal management requires careful prioritizing. The Leo can ask, "Which of these projects matters the most right now?" or "Which deadline is coming soonest?" They can then allocate time accordingly. Some tasks might be put on hold until more urgent projects are done.

It also helps to be realistic about how much energy they have. If they notice that all tasks together exceed their capacity, they might have to step back from something. This can be difficult for a driven Leo, but it prevents widespread burnout and ensures the goals they do keep remain at a high standard.

Adapting to Sudden Changes

In many projects, external factors can shift unexpectedly. A supplier might run out of materials, or a partner might drop from the project. Leos who are flexible can handle these surprises by quickly brainstorming new approaches. Their creative mindset can turn a sudden setback into a chance to try something else.

However, if a Leo is deeply attached to one perfect vision, they might struggle with last-minute changes. They could feel frustrated or disappointed. Learning to pivot can reduce stress. Instead of focusing on lost options, they can explore alternatives, possibly discovering a route that works even better than the original plan.

Communication is key when changes happen. The Leo should inform everyone involved about the new direction, gather feedback, and keep morale up. Their natural leadership can shine here if they remain calm and positive, guiding the team or themselves to adapt without losing hope.

Seeking Guidance and Learning from Mentors

Even the most confident Leo can benefit from the wisdom of those who have done similar projects before. Seeking a mentor, whether a teacher, a senior colleague, or a professional in the field, can give a Leo valuable shortcuts. Mentors can point out common mistakes, suggest tools, or share experiences that shed light on potential pitfalls.

This guidance does not diminish a Leo's pride. Instead, it shows maturity to learn from others and save time that might otherwise be spent on trial and error. A mentor can offer honest feedback, helping the Leo refine their ideas. It can also be helpful just to have someone who understands the field, especially if the project is complex.

Leos should remember to express appreciation to mentors. A simple thank-you or an update on how their advice helped can keep the relationship strong. Over time, the Leo might become a mentor too, passing on knowledge to newcomers. This flow of teaching and learning can enrich everyone involved.

Turning Projects into Ongoing Interests

Sometimes, a one-time project can spark a lasting interest. A Leo who tries designing a website might find they love web development and want to keep learning. A student who does a biology experiment might discover a passion for science. By noticing these sparks, Leos can shape future goals around them.

This might involve taking extra classes, joining clubs, or seeking side jobs in that field. Over time, hobbies can become careers, or side interests might evolve into main areas of expertise. Leos, with their natural enthusiasm, can thrive when they dive deeper into subjects that fascinate them.

It is also fine if a project remains a single event. Not every task has to become a lifelong path. If a Leo tries something and decides it is not for them, they can still walk away with new skills or understanding. That knowledge might come in handy later in unexpected ways.

Learning to Let Go of Perfection

Leos often have high standards for themselves. They might tweak details again and again, trying to achieve a flawless result. While aiming for excellence is good, an obsession with perfection can stall progress or cause extreme stress. It may even prevent them from finishing at all, as they keep seeing ways to improve.

A balanced mindset is to do the best they can within the time and resources available, then accept the result. They can remind themselves, "Done is better than endless tinkering." If there is more time after meeting the basic requirements, they can refine certain parts. But eventually, they must let the project stand.

Letting go of perfection also helps them move on to other goals. If they keep polishing one item forever, they might miss new opportunities. By understanding that every piece of work has room for improvement, they free themselves to keep learning and creating fresh things.

Recognizing the Value of Team Success

For Leos, it can be tempting to focus on personal glory. However, many important achievements happen through teamwork. When a group project succeeds, it is often because multiple people contributed unique skills. By acknowledging how each person's work mattered, a Leo can strengthen bonds and encourage future collaboration.

Team achievements can open doors. If a Leo participates in a group that wins a contest or develops a popular product, others will notice. Companies or schools might invite the team to take on bigger challenges. This means more recognition for everyone, including the Leo. By valuing group success as much as personal achievement, they expand their impact far beyond what they could do alone.

If friction arises in the team, a Leo can be the one to mend it by praising each person's efforts. Instead of pointing out who did less or who made mistakes, they can highlight how all members grew during the process. This kind of leadership builds trust and shows that the Leo is not just about self-promotion.

CHAPTER 9: HOW LEO DEALS WITH CHALLENGES

Leos are often described as strong, brave, and filled with energy. Yet, every person faces problems that can bring stress or fear, no matter how confident they usually feel. For Leos, challenges can show up in different parts of life: disagreements with friends or family, tough work projects, health worries, money concerns, or unexpected life changes. In this chapter, we will look at how Leos might respond to such difficulties. We will also discuss ways they can handle problems more effectively, all while staying true to their natural traits of boldness and warmth.

Acknowledging Feelings and Frustrations

When a Leo faces a problem, they may first feel shock or frustration. Because many Leos take pride in their ability to handle things, they might feel embarrassed or upset that they cannot fix the situation right away. For example, if a Leo suddenly loses a job, they may worry about what others will think or feel disappointed in themselves for not seeing the problem coming.

Despite these strong feelings, it is important for a Leo to allow themselves a moment to recognize what they are experiencing. They can think, "Yes, this situation is stressful, and it is okay to feel uneasy." By giving themselves time to notice their feelings, Leos can avoid pushing them aside. Hidden feelings can grow stronger later and cause bigger trouble if they are not dealt with. So, a short pause to admit, "I feel worried," or "I feel upset," is a good first step.

Leaning on Inner Strength

Leos are known for having a natural sense of bravery, which can help them stand up to challenges. Even when they feel worried, they often have the hidden energy to face problems head-on. This inner strength might be an advantage, but it can also lead them to take on too much at once. Leos may think, "I can solve this problem alone," without asking for help. Sometimes they do manage on their own, yet other times they might discover that a more balanced approach works better.

To use their strength wisely, Leos can remind themselves of times they overcame problems in the past. Thinking, "I have handled tough moments before, and I learned a lot from those times," helps them see that challenges are not always new or unbeatable. It also reminds them that they are not as powerless as they might feel.

However, Leos should also remember that true strength includes asking for support when it is needed. They might talk with friends, trusted family members, or even professionals. This does not mean they are weak; it means they are resourceful enough to gather the tools and knowledge that can help them. When they combine their own bravery with the guidance of others, they can tackle problems with greater confidence.

Avoiding Sudden Anger

When problems arise, Leos may react with fast, strong emotions. Sometimes, their frustration can show as anger. For instance, if a Leo feels they have been treated unfairly, they might raise their voice or speak harshly. While it is normal to feel mad about injustice, reacting too quickly can push people away. It may also lead to choices that the Leo regrets later.

A helpful tip is to pause and take a breath before acting. If a Leo notices they are about to say something hurtful or make a rushed decision, they can think, "Let me wait just a moment." Taking a bit of time to calm down can prevent damage to relationships or the situation itself. In that short pause, they can also ask themselves, "Will this action actually help fix the problem?" If the answer is no, they can find a different approach.

Another way to lessen anger is to explore healthier outlets. Some Leos might find that physical activity, such as going for a jog or doing a simple exercise routine, helps them let off steam in a safe way. Others might write in a journal or draw pictures. These methods can release strong feelings without directing them at other people. Once the Leo feels calmer, they can come back to the issue with a clearer mind.

Breaking Problems into Parts

Some challenges look huge at first. For example, if a Leo has money worries or a massive work task, they might feel buried under the weight of it. This can lead to stress, panic, or avoidance. One helpful method is to split the big problem into smaller parts. This strategy can give a Leo a sense of control, since each small step is more manageable than one giant leap.

Let's say a Leo needs to pay off a large debt or finish a big creative project. Instead of trying to fix the whole situation in one move, they can list smaller tasks. Perhaps they make a weekly budget or plan how many pages they will write per day. Each time they handle one small part, they can check it off and notice real progress. This helps maintain motivation over time.

Because Leos can sometimes be impatient, they may want quick results. Breaking things into parts teaches them patience and shows them that steady work often leads to better outcomes than rushing.

By going step by step, Leos can keep their eyes on the process instead of feeling hopeless about a tough situation.

Seeking Trusted Advice

Leos might feel tempted to hide problems out of pride. They may worry that asking for help will make them look weak. But in truth, reaching out to a trusted mentor, friend, or professional is a sign of clear thinking. We all benefit from another person's viewpoint now and then, especially if that person has experience with similar issues.

If a Leo feels stuck, they can think of someone they respect. That might be a parent, an older relative, a teacher, a friend who has gone through similar troubles, or a support group. By explaining the situation, Leos can learn new tips. For example, if they are dealing with a challenge at work, they might speak with a colleague who has faced the same problem. If they are having a problem in a friendship, they might talk with someone who has known them both for a long time.

Leos do not need to follow every piece of advice they get. Instead, they can gather ideas and see which ones fit best. The choice to accept or reject certain suggestions remains in their hands. Often, though, a little outside insight makes a big difference.

Using Creativity to Solve Problems

Leos tend to have lively imaginations, which can be a big help in solving problems. For example, if a Leo faces conflict with a classmate or coworker, they might find a creative way to apologize or break the tension, such as writing a kind note or suggesting a simple group activity that rebuilds trust. If a Leo is stuck on a project, they might brainstorm out-of-the-box ideas that set them apart from others.

This creative approach can keep challenges from feeling too heavy. Rather than getting stuck in a dull or rigid mindset, Leos can experiment with different solutions. They might sketch out plans, draft outlines, or act out possible conversations to see which outcome feels right. This playful, imaginative style can bring fresh life into an otherwise grim situation.

Still, Leos should stay alert that creativity alone is not enough if they do not also take real steps to handle the core issue. It is one thing to dream up interesting solutions, but those solutions must also be realistic. By blending their creative spark with practical actions, Leos can discover answers that might not be obvious to others.

Strengthening Focus

When a big challenge appears, it is easy for a Leo to let their mind jump from one worry to another. They might think of many fears at once, which can add to their stress. Learning to strengthen focus can help. For instance, they might set aside time each day to work on just one part of the problem, ignoring all other distractions. This can be as short as 20 or 30 minutes of solid focus.

During this time, they can turn off social media or find a quiet place to think. They might note down possible solutions or take action steps without letting their attention wander. Then, after that set time, they can stop and rest or do something else. This focused period can lead to noticeable progress over the days and weeks, especially if they are facing a complicated challenge.

Focus can also apply to emotional issues. If a Leo is upset about a relationship conflict, they can spend a set amount of time thinking calmly about it, writing down reasons for the conflict and possible ways to fix it. After that time, they put it aside, trusting that they will come back to it later. By focusing in short bursts, they avoid constant worry throughout the day.

Accepting That Not Everything Can Be Controlled

Leos often like to be in charge of events around them. While that works in many situations, life has plenty of surprises no one can control. For example, someone might lose their job because of changes in a company, or a natural event might alter their plans. In these moments, a Leo can feel helpless or angry that their hard work did not stop the unwanted event.

Learning to accept that some parts of life are out of our hands is tough but necessary. Instead of blaming themselves or others, Leos can focus on what they can change. If the challenge is caused by outside forces, they can still choose how they react. Do they allow it to break their spirit, or do they adapt and find a new path?

This acceptance does not mean giving up. It simply means using their energy in areas they can actually impact. If a Leo realizes a certain door is closed, they can start looking for other doors that might be open. This shift in mindset often makes challenges feel less like personal failures and more like directions to explore different routes.

Learning from Setbacks

When something goes wrong, Leos might feel bitter or upset at first. However, setbacks can hold valuable lessons. If a plan falls apart, a Leo might ask, "What could I do better next time?" or "What warning signs did I miss?" Reflecting on these points can prevent the same mistake from happening again.

This reflection should not turn into blaming themselves harshly. Instead, it should be seen as a chance to grow. If a Leo attempted a personal project and it failed, they can note if they needed better time management, clearer goals, or more help. Then, for the next project, they can fix those errors. Over many challenges, this habit of learning can shape a Leo into someone who is stronger and wiser.

Additionally, thinking back on past successes can also be helpful. A Leo might recall how they tackled another hard issue some time ago and came out fine. That memory can boost their faith in themselves. The trick is to balance looking at past slips with also recalling moments of strength, building a well-rounded sense of confidence.

Handling Pressure from Others

Sometimes, challenges come not from our own goals but from other people's expectations. A Leo might feel pressure to perform at work, keep up with high-achieving friends, or fulfill family wishes. While Leos often enjoy impressing those around them, too much pressure can become stressful. They could worry about disappointing others, which adds extra weight to the challenge they are already facing.

In these cases, a Leo can decide whose opinions truly matter. Are these voices supportive or critical without reason? If friends or family constantly push them without understanding the Leo's situation, it might be wise for the Leo to set boundaries. For example, they can politely say, "I value your thoughts, but I need space to handle this in my own way." Setting limits does not mean they do not care; it means they are trying to keep a healthier balance.

Leos should also remember they do not have to take on everyone's problems or wishes. If a request is too big, they can explain why it is not possible at the moment. While Leos often want to be seen as dependable, they do not owe everyone a yes. Saying no or asking for more time is sometimes the best move for the Leo's well-being.

Building Resilience Through Healthy Routines

When life feels rough, having a stable routine can keep a person steady. For Leos, this might include regular sleep patterns, simple exercise, and balanced eating. It may sound small, but these basics can make a difference in how well someone handles stress. A tired or hungry Leo might react more strongly to bad news than one who feels rested and fed.

Routines can also include short breaks for breathing exercises or calm reflection. Taking five minutes to breathe quietly can reset the mind during a tough day. Some Leos might enjoy short walks outside, even around the block, to clear their heads. Others may prefer gentle stretching. These small habits can lower stress, making challenges feel less scary.

Additionally, setting a regular schedule for tasks can help a Leo avoid last-minute rushes. If they spread out their work or chores across the week, they reduce the chance of feeling swamped. That way, when a new challenge appears, they have some space to handle it without completely rearranging their life.

Using Humor and Positivity Wisely

Leos often have a bright sense of humor that can lighten up tense moments. Even in trouble, they might find a witty comment or see a funny side. This can help them (and those around them) stay hopeful. Laughter can release tension and remind everyone that problems, while serious, do not have to crush our spirit.

However, Leos should be careful not to use humor as a way to avoid facing real issues. If a problem is big or deeply painful, constant jokes can seem insensitive or out of place. The best approach is to balance humor with honesty. They might share a light remark to ease the heaviness, but still acknowledge the core issue. This combination can keep morale up without pretending the challenge does not exist.

Positivity is also useful, but only if it is rooted in reality. Saying, "Everything will be okay" when there is no plan might not be as helpful as saying, "We can work through this step by step, and we'll find a way." That second statement admits there is work to do, which is often more reassuring in the long run.

Knowing When to Let Go

Sometimes, a challenge involves something a Leo dearly wants, like a specific job, relationship, or outcome. Yet, no matter what they do, it might not turn out as hoped. In these moments, it can be heartbreaking for a Leo to let go, because they feel their identity is connected to that dream or plan.

Letting go does not mean a Leo is a quitter. Instead, it can show wisdom. If an ongoing effort causes constant pain or leads nowhere, a Leo might decide to free themselves from that path and direct their energy to a better one. This can open the door to new opportunities that fit them more.

For example, if a relationship is full of hurtful interactions and cannot be fixed, stepping away might protect the Leo's well-being. If a job no longer matches their values or skills, moving on might let them find work that respects their abilities. While it can be tough to say goodbye to something familiar, the relief that follows can bring a sense of fresh purpose.

Staying True to Personal Values

When facing trouble, it can be tempting to bend one's moral or personal standards just to get a quick solution. A Leo might feel pressured to lie, cheat, or act in ways that do not match their usual principles. But in the long run, this usually causes more issues, like guilt or bigger consequences down the line.

Holding onto values means seeking solutions that are fair and honest, even if they take longer. This approach protects a Leo's self-respect. If a business challenge appears, a Leo who stays honest and keeps promises may earn trust from coworkers or customers. If a social challenge appears, a Leo who remains loyal and truthful may keep their good name intact.

This does not mean Leos have to be perfect. Mistakes happen under stress. But if they sense they are acting against what they believe is right, they can pause and reconsider. Returning to a path that respects their core values usually builds stronger self-esteem, which can help them face future challenges more confidently.

Supporting Others While Facing Personal Problems

A caring Leo might still want to help others even when they are dealing with their own troubles. In some cases, giving support to a friend or family member can bring a sense of purpose and take the focus away from their own stress. It might remind them that everyone struggles, and we can lift each other.

However, Leos must be cautious not to ignore their own needs. If they are too busy taking care of everyone else, they may have little energy left for their own issues. This can lead to burnout. Finding a balance between helping others and handling personal problems is key. They can do small acts of support without sacrificing their own well-being.

If a Leo finds it hard to say no to others, they can practice phrases like, "I wish I could, but I am dealing with something big right now," or "I can help you for a little while, but I need some time for my own tasks too." Most reasonable people will understand. If someone does not, that might be a sign the relationship is one-sided, and the Leo should be careful about how much they give.

Speaking Up for Fairness

If a challenge comes from unfair treatment, Leos might be quick to call it out. They can stand up for themselves or for others who are mistreated. This might mean writing a letter to a higher-up in the workplace, talking to a school official, or gathering support from peers. Speaking up can bring a sense of empowerment, letting a Leo feel they are not just sitting back and accepting something wrong.

However, speaking up effectively requires thought. A Leo who comes in yelling might cause people to become defensive, which makes it harder to fix the issue. A calmer, fact-based approach often works better. They might list the unfair behavior, explain why it is harmful, and propose ways to make it right. That way, they show they are serious and reasonable.

By doing this, Leos also help set a standard for fairness. Others might see their actions and feel inspired to stand against injustice too. This can create a better environment for everyone, which might reduce the chance of such challenges arising again.

Turning Challenges into Opportunities to Grow Skills

Whether the challenge is personal, social, or professional, Leos can use it as a chance to sharpen skills they did not focus on before. For example, if they are struggling with time management, they can learn new techniques or use tools like planners or apps. If they are facing a conflict with someone, they can improve communication skills or learn ways to negotiate calmly.

Viewing challenges as skill-building exercises changes the mood. Instead of thinking, "This problem is ruining my life," Leos can think,

"I can practice new methods here that might help me in the future." That switch in perspective can reduce anxiety, because it sees the situation as a learning moment rather than just a disaster.

Over many years, these small bits of learning add up, making Leos more capable. Each problem faced gives them more insight and a wider range of approaches to try next time.

Handling Health-Related Problems

Health troubles—physical or emotional—can feel especially scary. A Leo might be used to feeling strong, so any sickness or emotional problem can shake their confidence. In these times, they should remember that seeking professional help is wise. Talking with a doctor, counselor, or therapist does not mean giving up. It shows that they are serious about caring for themselves.

Leos might also use their natural determination to follow through with health routines, such as regular check-ups or therapy sessions. It might be tempting to skip these appointments if they feel discouraged, but consistency can lead to better results. And if a particular treatment or method is not helping, they can speak with the professional to adjust it. This open communication often leads to better outcomes.

Friends and family support can also help a Leo with health worries. A positive environment, along with proper care, might speed up recovery or lessen emotional strain. Because Leos often like to protect loved ones from seeing them weak, they may hesitate to ask for help. Yet, letting caring people share the burden can make the challenge easier to carry.

CHAPTER 10: HOW LEO EXPRESSES CREATIVITY

Leos are known for their flair, drama, and fiery energy. When these traits come together, they often turn into many forms of creative expression. Whether in art, music, performance, writing, or simple day-to-day acts, Leos can channel their bright spirits into something unique. In this chapter, we will look at the various ways Leos might show creativity, why they enjoy expressing themselves, and how they can develop these skills in a healthy way. We will also see that creativity for a Leo is not only about making things look pretty—it can be about solving problems, sharing ideas, and connecting with the people around them.

Natural Desire to Stand Out

One reason Leos often explore creative outlets is their tendency to enjoy being noticed. In art, music, or writing, a person can present a part of themselves that others do not usually see. For example, a Leo might paint a large, bright-colored mural or write a powerful story that reflects their internal emotions. Because they relish the chance to show their talents, creative work can feel like a perfect fit.

However, self-expression is not always about seeking attention. It can also be a way for Leos to process their own feelings and ideas. The results might be bold or playful, reflecting their natural spark. Even a small activity, such as decorating a personal space or cooking an eye-catching meal, can become an art form for a Leo who wants to stand out.

Sometimes, though, they might feel pressured to keep producing big, showy pieces. It is important for them to remember that creativity can be quiet, too. A poem in a notebook or a personal scrapbook can be just as meaningful as a loud performance. Balancing the public side of creation with personal satisfaction can keep Leos from burning out.

Love for Performing Arts

Many Leos are drawn to performing arts, such as theater, dance, or singing. These areas allow them to channel their energy in front of an audience. The stage lights, applause, and sense of excitement can be thrilling. A Leo might feel a rush when the curtains open, knowing that all eyes are on them.

In dance, they might pour their passion into each movement. In theater, they can use their boldness to fill a character with life. In singing or playing music, they express feelings through melody or rhythm. This kind of creativity lets a Leo explore different sides of themselves. They might find joy in portraying a comedic role one night and a dramatic role another time.

Yet, stage performance can also come with nerves or self-doubt. Even confident Leos might worry about forgetting lines or hitting a wrong note. Learning to handle these worries can be part of the creative process, reminding Leos that mistakes are normal. Supportive teachers, directors, or fellow performers can help them keep going. Over time, each performance becomes a learning step, sharpening their skills.

Artistic Expression Through Visual Media

Beyond the stage, Leos may find joy in painting, drawing, sculpture, or digital design. These mediums let them use color, shape, and style to share ideas. A Leo's artwork might feature bright shades, large shapes, or dramatic contrasts. They might enjoy painting large canvases that reflect their grand inner vision.

Visual creativity can also appear in more everyday tasks. For instance, some Leos have a knack for putting together stylish outfits or decorating their home with a personal flair. They might arrange furniture or choose color themes that create a warm, welcoming environment. This natural sense of design can make their surroundings feel lively and original.

When using visual art for personal expression, Leos do not need to aim for complete perfection. If they find themselves worried about every line or shade being flawless, they might lose the fun of creation. Instead, it can help to see art as a way to explore, not just impress. Some Leos might even keep a sketchbook where they doodle ideas or try new techniques, allowing them to enjoy the process without constant pressure.

Creating Through Words

Words can be a strong tool for Leos. Some might find that writing poems, stories, or songs helps them share their thoughts. Because many Leos are full of feeling, writing can be a natural outlet. They might use dramatic language or powerful images to convey what is in their hearts. This can lead to storytelling that captures readers' attention.

Even in more formal writing, like articles or blog posts, Leos can bring a lively tone. They might enjoy choosing interesting phrases or weaving in humor. If they are passionate about a topic—be it sports, a social cause, or a personal hobby—their writing can radiate excitement.

However, like any creative path, writing requires practice. A Leo may want immediate praise for their words, yet real skill often develops slowly. By writing daily, revising drafts, and studying the work of better writers, a Leo can refine their style. If they stick with it, they might find that their voice becomes increasingly clear and powerful.

Finding Inspiration Everywhere

Leos have an eye for drama and beauty in the world around them. They might notice a striking sunset or a conversation in a coffee shop that sparks an idea for a painting or story. This willingness to see something special in everyday life can feed their creativity constantly.

Some Leos keep a small notebook or use a phone app to record sparks of inspiration. That way, if they hear a funny phrase or see a new color combination in nature, they can note it down for later use. Because their minds are often active, these moments can build up into a store of creative fuel.

At the same time, it is easy for anyone to overlook simple wonders when life gets busy. A Leo can keep their creativity alive by pausing to observe details around them: the shape of leaves, the pattern of shadows, or the laughter of children. These small things might lead to fresh ideas for art, writing, or another creative project.

Group Creativity and Collaboration

While some forms of creativity happen alone, Leos may also enjoy working with a group. Their leadership traits can help unite people around a shared goal, such as a group art show, a play, or a music band. With their warm and enthusiastic nature, they can build excitement among teammates.

However, this approach requires the Leo to practice listening. Collaboration means blending ideas, not just following one person's vision. If a Leo tries to control every detail, others might feel unappreciated. By asking, "What do you think?" or "How can we combine these ideas?" the Leo ensures everyone feels involved.

Group creativity can also help Leos learn new skills. They might pick up painting tricks from a teammate or discover a new style of music from a friend. Sharing knowledge often leads to unexpected outcomes. The end product might be far different—and sometimes better—than what a single person could do alone.

Turning Tasks into Something Fun

Leos can bring a creative touch even to mundane tasks. For example, if they must organize an office or arrange a schedule, they might turn it into a visual chart with color codes and little drawings. If they host a get-together at home, they might add interesting centerpieces or a fun activity that surprises guests.

This habit of turning ordinary duties into mini art projects can help them stay motivated. It keeps boredom away and lets them see daily life as a place for creative sparks. Friends and family might also look forward to seeing what clever twist the Leo will add next.

Still, there is a risk of spending too long perfecting minor details, which can slow down actual completion of tasks. A balance is helpful. If the job is time-sensitive, a Leo should focus on getting it done first, then add small creative touches only if time allows. This way, creativity remains a pleasant addition rather than a barrier.

Inventive Problem-Solving

Creativity is not only about art or performance. Leos can use their bright minds to find new solutions to everyday problems. For instance, if a group of friends cannot agree on where to meet, a Leo might come up with a clever location or a way to share travel. If a workplace procedure seems slow, they might suggest a method that speeds it up while keeping it interesting.

By seeing problems as puzzles rather than roadblocks, Leos often enjoy experimenting with unusual angles. This might mean writing down different ideas, even if some seem silly, to find a hidden gem. It could also mean mixing two methods that people do not normally combine. Because they do not fear attention, they are sometimes willing to propose ideas that others might consider too risky.

Of course, not every idea will succeed. But having a creative attitude means Leos will keep searching until they find something that works. Over time, this willingness to test new solutions can make them stand out as innovators in a class, a job, or a community project.

Confidence and the Spotlight

Leos often enjoy showing the result of their creativity. Whether it is a painting, a short film, a piece of music, or even a written essay, they might look for ways to share it with an audience. This desire to be seen can push them to polish their work. They might spend extra time improving certain parts because they want everything to shine.

On the flip side, wanting recognition can become a problem if they depend too much on applause. If they do not receive the reaction they hoped for, they might feel deflated. Learning to create for personal satisfaction first can keep their spirits strong. Applause becomes a bonus, not the only reason to make something.

This approach also helps if they face critique. Not everyone will love a Leo's work. Rather than feeling crushed by negative comments, they can use them as helpful feedback. If the critique is fair, they can adapt and learn. If it is overly harsh or unkind, they can remember that they still find worth in what they made, regardless of one person's view.

Finding Time to Explore New Ideas

Busy schedules can limit how much space a Leo has to be creative. Work, school, and daily tasks might leave them too tired to try new ideas. Yet, creativity often thrives when there is a bit of free space. A Leo might set aside small time blocks—maybe 15 minutes a day or one hour a week—to do something purely creative.

During this time, they should let themselves experiment without worrying about the final result. They might doodle, write random thoughts, or play with a musical instrument. Freed from the pressure to produce something perfect, they can discover new possibilities. Sometimes, these unplanned experiments spark big projects later.

It can also help to find or create a personal corner or a room for creative work. If a Leo has a small desk or area to keep their supplies, they can jump into art or writing more quickly. Keeping the tools visible can remind them to spend a few minutes exploring ideas whenever they get the chance.

Sharing with a Community

Whether online or in person, creative communities can give Leos a place to display their work and see what others are making. There might be local craft fairs, open-mic nights, or online forums where people post drawings or videos. By joining these spaces, Leos can get supportive feedback and ideas. They might also meet potential collaborators or mentors.

Being part of such a community also teaches Leos that creativity is a shared experience. They might see someone else's painting style and feel inspired to learn a new technique. They might read stories that give them different viewpoints. This interaction can expand their own creative palette, making their work richer and more varied.

However, engaging with a community comes with the possibility of comparing themselves to others. Leos might see someone else's success and feel jealous or inadequate. To keep a healthy mindset, they can remember that creativity is not a race. Everyone has a distinct path. Applauding others' achievements can bring unity, and learning from their methods can spark personal growth.

The Role of Emotions

Leos feel emotions strongly, and creativity can be a channel for all that feeling. If a Leo is joyful, they might paint sunny landscapes or write energetic songs. If they are sad, they might create softer, more thoughtful pieces. Anger could drive them to produce fiery art with bold colors, or to write poems that vent frustration.

Using creativity to handle emotions is often healthier than hiding them. Writing a poem or song about a problem might help the Leo make sense of it. Painting their feelings might allow them to see patterns they did not notice before. By expressing emotions in this way, they can release some tension and perhaps find answers within their own work.

At the same time, being creative when upset can lead to dramatic works that might surprise or even unsettle others. Leos should decide whether they want to share such personal pieces. It is okay to keep some creations private if they contain very sensitive parts of themselves. The main goal is to let those emotions move through in a productive way rather than letting them stay bottled up.

Overcoming Creative Blocks

Even the most imaginative Leo can run into creative blocks, times when no new ideas seem to come. This can be frustrating for someone used to feeling full of spark. Some blocks might be caused by stress, lack of rest, or too much pressure to make something "perfect."

A helpful step is to step away from the problem. A Leo might go for a short walk, read a book in a totally different field, or chat with a friend about unrelated topics. These activities can refresh the mind, allowing new ideas to pop up later. Trying a different creative activity can also help. If a Leo is stuck on writing, they might try painting or making crafts. Switching mediums might unlock fresh thinking.

Sometimes, simply making something small and imperfect can break the block. A Leo might doodle random shapes or write a quick silly story without caring if it is any good. That removes the pressure and reminds them that creativity can be playful. Once they feel relaxed, bigger ideas might flow more easily.

Teaching Others

Leos who have honed their creative abilities might enjoy passing on their knowledge. Whether they are showing a younger sibling how to draw or teaching a friend some guitar chords, they can share their enthusiasm. By explaining techniques to someone else, they might notice new details about their art form and become better at it themselves.

Teaching also gives a sense of purpose. A Leo may find it fulfilling to see another person discover their own creative spark. This builds bonds and spreads positivity. However, teachers need patience. Not everyone learns at the same speed, and some might have different styles. By listening and adapting, a Leo can become an effective guide.

If teaching in a formal setting, like a workshop, a Leo should plan sessions so they are both fun and informative. Because they have a natural flair for performance, they can keep lessons exciting. Including hands-on practice, friendly feedback, and group interactions can make everyone feel included.

Handling Criticism

When a Leo shares creative work, it may draw a range of reactions. While some feedback might be supportive, others could be negative or even harsh. This can hurt if a Leo poured their heart into the piece. But learning to handle criticism is part of the creative journey. Not every voice will understand a Leo's style or message.

Before reacting, it helps to consider who is giving the feedback and why. If it is a trusted friend or a mentor offering thoughtful suggestions, the Leo can learn from it. If it is someone just being rude without reason, the Leo can discard it. Either way, it does not define their worth as an artist or person.

Keeping an open mind to well-meant tips can make a Leo's work stronger. They might improve composition, refine their writing, or adjust a performance technique. At the same time, they should hold onto their unique vision. They do not have to change everything just to please critics. Finding a healthy balance between self-assurance and willingness to grow is key.

Balancing Creativity with Daily Life

Since creativity can be exciting, a Leo might spend hours on a project and forget about other duties. While this can lead to impressive results, it may also create problems if they skip important tasks. Over time, letting life get out of balance can cause stress. A Leo might lose track of homework, job responsibilities, or basic self-care.

A simple plan, like making a schedule, can help. They can set clear times for creative work and other times for chores, rest, and social activities. This structure ensures they do not neglect important areas of life. Ironically, having some boundaries often makes creativity flow more because the Leo is not weighed down by guilt or undone tasks.

They can also combine creativity with responsibilities. For example, if they have a big presentation at work, they might use art or humor to make it more engaging. That way, they satisfy both their creative urges and their real-world goals. This practical blend helps them shine in all areas of life, rather than feeling pulled in two directions.

Staying Inspired Long-Term

Creativity is not a one-time event. Many Leos want to keep expressing themselves as they grow older. That might mean shifting interests or mediums over time. Someone who wrote poems in high school might discover a love for photography later in life. Embracing these changes can keep the Leo's creative spark alive.

Exploring new skills or collaborating with people who have different talents can also fight boredom. If a Leo always sings alone, they might join a choir. If they have always drawn, maybe they try sculpting. Each fresh experience can recharge their excitement. They also gather new ideas that might spark breakthroughs in their usual art form.

Reading books, attending events, and watching documentaries can also feed their minds with fresh input. Sometimes, stepping away from creating to absorb new viewpoints can lead to big leaps in skill or style. The main goal is to stay curious and open, never assuming they have learned all there is to know.

Creative Problem-Solving in Relationships

Leos might use their creative mindset to nurture personal relationships. Rather than following the same routines, they can plan interesting ways to spend time with family or friends. This could be creating a mini talent show at home, writing funny letters to a friend far away, or cooking an unusual meal together.

If conflicts occur, creative communication might help mend them. A Leo might write a heartfelt note or design a small token of apology rather than just saying sorry. They could also suggest a game that encourages everyone to talk things out in a fun manner. These approaches can soften tension, since they show thoughtfulness and a willingness to make things better.

It is important to remember that not all people respond equally to creative gestures. Some friends or relatives might prefer direct conversation or a calm approach. A Leo can observe how the other person feels. If a certain method does not help, they can try another. Creativity, matched with empathy, can open the door to better understanding.

Encouraging Confidence in Others

Leos may also use creativity to boost the confidence of those around them. They can form small art clubs, writing circles, or music sessions where everyone feels free to share. Because of their natural warmth, they can make group members feel safe even if someone is shy. Celebrating others' work can help them see that everyone has something to offer.

By shining the spotlight on others sometimes, a Leo builds a community where each person's voice matters. This also reflects well on the Leo, showing they are not just hungry for their own attention. Over time, this approach can lead to lasting friendships and networks that keep creativity alive in everyone involved.

Finding Personal Meaning in Creativity

At the heart of it all, creativity for a Leo is about expressing their inner light. Whether they paint, dance, write, cook, design, or invent, they are sharing a piece of themselves. This act can bring deep personal satisfaction, helping them know themselves better. It can also give others a glimpse into the Leo's mind and heart, building stronger connections.

While Leos might enjoy the external praise that comes from creative work, they should not forget the inner benefits: understanding their emotions, learning new skills, and feeling the joy of making something out of nothing. Even if no one else sees a particular piece of art or hears a piece of music, the act of creating can be its own reward.

Over time, many Leos find that their creative ventures shape their identity. They might explore different styles or methods as they mature. The main thread remains the same: a powerful desire to express the warmth and strength they carry inside. Through practice, collaboration, and a spirit of exploration, they craft not just objects or performances, but also a richer sense of who they are. And that, in the end, may be the greatest gift creativity offers them.

CHAPTER 11: LEO AND PERSONAL GROWTH

Leos are often linked with confidence, leadership, and a fiery spirit. While these qualities can set them apart, they also influence how Leos approach growing as individuals. Personal growth is a long-term process that involves learning more about oneself, forming healthy habits, and adapting to life changes. For Leos, this growth can be shaped by their desire to shine, help others, and remain true to their natural strengths. In this chapter, we will explore how Leos may develop new skills, handle setbacks, and deepen their sense of self in a way that respects their passionate nature.

Understanding the Drive to Improve

From a young age, Leos may feel a pull to move beyond basic expectations. This can show up in school, friendships, or extracurricular activities. They might step forward to lead a group project, feeling energized by the chance to stand out. As they get older, many Leos retain this drive and look for paths to enhance their talents, knowledge, or relationships.

A key part of growth is recognizing that there is always more to learn. While a Leo might start off believing in their natural gifts, they soon discover that raw talent alone does not guarantee success. For instance, a Leo who excels at public speaking might initially rely on strong delivery and presence. Over time, they see that careful preparation, research, and empathy for the audience can elevate their impact even more.

Accepting this idea—that growth is ongoing—can help Leos remain open to new input. By telling themselves, "I can become better if I stay curious," they maintain a healthy sense of progress. It keeps them from settling into a routine where they assume they have already reached the top.

Learning Self-Reflection

Self-reflection is a powerful tool for personal growth, but it may not come naturally to every Leo. Because many Leos prefer action and external engagement, they might find it tricky to pause and look inward. Yet, regular self-reflection can reveal patterns, good and bad, that shape how they act and relate to others.

Some Leos might use a journal to capture daily events or feelings. Others may find a few quiet minutes before bedtime to think, "What went well today? What did not go as I hoped?" They might ask themselves if they handled a conflict effectively or if they met their personal standards in a certain task. This practice can offer a clearer understanding of their choices and the outcomes.

Self-reflection can also help Leos notice times when pride hinders them. For instance, a Leo might see they brushed off a helpful suggestion because they felt they knew best. Acknowledging that moment allows them to improve next time. They might say, "I realize I shut down that idea too quickly. I will be more open in the future." Such small insights guide bigger personal changes.

Balancing Confidence with Humility

One challenge for Leos is to keep their innate self-assurance while avoiding a sense of superiority. Confidence is one of their strengths, helping them move forward with courage. But if it tilts into arrogance or constant need for praise, it can block growth. After all, people who think they know everything often miss valuable lessons.

Humility does not mean discarding self-esteem. Instead, it means knowing that everyone has areas to improve and that no one is right all the time. Leos can practice humility by listening actively when someone shares feedback. If a friend says, "I felt left out when you took control," the Leo can pause and think about whether they pushed too hard. Instead of snapping back, they might say, "I did not realize that. Tell me more."

Balancing confidence with humility fosters a welcoming atmosphere where others feel comfortable offering ideas. That, in turn, can accelerate a Leo's personal growth. They learn from different views, refine their skills, and avoid the trap of repeating the same mistakes. Over time, they become leaders who inspire rather than intimidate.

Building Emotional Awareness

Emotional awareness is another layer of personal development. Leos often have strong feelings, but they might not always interpret them calmly. They can be quick to express joy, anger, or excitement. These intense emotions can be a source of warmth and connection, yet they can also cause problems if they flare up unchecked.

Developing emotional awareness includes noticing what triggers certain reactions. For instance, a Leo might notice that they get frustrated when plans change at the last minute. Understanding that trigger allows them to prepare mentally. The next time a last-minute change occurs, they can remind themselves, "I usually dislike sudden changes, but let's see if we can adapt smoothly." This shifts their response from instant anger to measured problem-solving.

Also, emotional awareness involves learning to name feelings. Instead of saying, "I am upset," they can specify, "I feel disappointed because my work was overlooked." This detail helps them address the core issue instead of lashing out. A Leo who can clearly express sadness, frustration, or excitement is better equipped to communicate with friends, relatives, and coworkers, reducing misunderstandings.

Goal-Setting and Achievement

Because Leos tend to be ambitious, goal-setting can shape their personal growth. They might set targets for physical fitness, academic performance, career progress, or relationship improvements. Having concrete aims can keep them focused, especially when life gets busy.

However, it helps to keep these goals realistic and broken into steps. For example, if a Leo wants to improve their public speaking, they might set sub-goals like watching one speech per day online, practicing a short talk each weekend, and joining a local speaking group. Each step is specific and measurable, giving them small wins along the way.

Regular check-ins support this process. A Leo might review their progress every month. If they see they are meeting milestones smoothly, they can stick with their plan. If they are lagging, they can adjust their approach rather than giving up. Over time, they refine both their aims and their methods, growing in confidence and skill.

Learning to Handle Setbacks

Personal growth often includes setbacks. Even the most talented Leo will face moments when they fail to reach a goal, lose an opportunity, or face rejection. At first, their pride might sting. However, setbacks are not the end of the road; they can be lessons in disguise.

When a plan fails, a Leo can use reflection to figure out what happened. Maybe they depended too heavily on one approach or did not prepare enough. Or perhaps the failure was caused by outside factors nobody could control. Recognizing the difference between internal and external reasons for a setback can help them respond wisely. If the issue is internal, they can change their approach next time. If it is external, they can look for alternative paths.

Patience is also vital here. Leos like to see swift results, but growth does not always move quickly. If they keep an open mind and persevere through difficulties, they build resilience. Over time, those tough moments can fuel a sense of self-trust, because they learn they can handle challenges without losing hope.

Expanding Knowledge and Skills

While many see Leos as natural leaders or performers, they can develop in many other areas if they remain curious. For instance, a Leo might explore technology, science, cooking, or any field that sparks their interest. Studying new subjects broadens their perspective and may reveal talents they never noticed.

Exploration can happen in small ways. Leos might watch educational videos, read books, or attend workshops. They might talk to people with different interests, asking questions to uncover fresh insights. By stepping outside their comfort zone, they challenge themselves to grow in unexpected directions.

As they learn, Leos may also feel the urge to share newfound knowledge. Teaching or mentoring others can reinforce their own learning, since explaining ideas demands clear understanding. The more they master new skills, the more confident and versatile they become. This can strengthen their sense of purpose and open doors in both personal and professional areas.

Nurturing Supportive Relationships

Part of personal growth for Leos involves building healthy relationships with family, friends, and mentors. While Leos can thrive on attention, they need to be sure their bonds are based on real care, not just admiration. When Leos connect with people who like them for who they truly are—both the bright and the vulnerable sides—they have a solid foundation for growth.

These supportive individuals might be the ones who offer honest feedback, cheer on the Leo's efforts, or step in when they see harmful patterns. For instance, a caring friend might point out if the Leo is overworking, ignoring their well-being in the rush to succeed. Because the friend truly cares, the Leo is more likely to listen.

Also, having someone who celebrates small improvements with them is a big boost. Whether it is a sibling applauding a new personal best at the gym or a mentor acknowledging the Leo's improved leadership style, these gestures let the Leo feel recognized. Positive reinforcement can encourage them to keep going, even when the path is not easy.

Managing Stress and Finding Balance

Leos pour a lot of energy into whatever they do, which can lead to stress if they do not pace themselves. Personal growth includes learning to balance effort with rest. Overcommitting can burn them out, reducing their effectiveness in all areas.

Finding balance might mean scheduling time for hobbies, relaxation, or simply being with friends without an agenda. A Leo can reflect on their typical week: Do they leave space for a mental breather? If the answer is no, they might set aside certain hours for walking, reading, or listening to calm music.

Stress management also involves recognizing warning signs, such as headaches, irritability, or disrupted sleep. If a Leo sees these signs, they can step back, reevaluate their workload, and set clearer limits. This adjustment is not a sign of weakness. In fact, it is a wise move that helps them stay strong in the long run.

Contributing to the Community

Growth is not just about bettering oneself; it can also include helping others in meaningful ways. Many Leos feel drawn to community involvement. They might volunteer, organize events, or advocate for causes they believe in. These activities let them use their leadership and warmth to benefit others.

This outward focus can enrich the Leo's sense of purpose. It reminds them that success is not solely about personal gain. Giving time or resources to help neighbors or broader social groups teaches empathy. It also challenges Leos to see problems from different angles. Through service, they might discover new personal insights that deepen their own understanding of life.

Such community involvement can connect them with like-minded people who share their passion for making a difference. Working side by side with others on a project builds friendships and fosters collaboration skills. As Leos see the tangible results of their efforts—like a park cleaned up or a local drive completed—they feel proud in a grounded way, not just for shining themselves but for lifting others too.

Being Open to Change and Adaptation

Life constantly changes, and for a Leo set in a certain routine, that can be disconcerting. Yet, personal growth often demands flexibility. If a career path shifts, a Leo might need to learn new skills or move to a different area. If a relationship dynamic changes, they might need to adjust their communication style.

By viewing change as a natural process rather than a threat, Leos can adapt with more ease. They might say to themselves, "Things are different now, so how can I respond in a constructive way?" This mindset turns fear into curiosity, and frustration into problem-solving.

Adaptation can bring unexpected gains. A Leo who must switch careers might discover a hidden passion in the new field. One who moves to a new city might meet friends they would never have encountered otherwise. Openness to change keeps them from clinging to old ways that no longer serve them, allowing fresh opportunities to unfold.

Reflecting on Values and Direction

As Leos evolve, they might revisit what truly matters to them. Early on, they may focus on external success—praise, awards, or positions of power. Later, they may realize they value honesty, kindness, or creativity more deeply than material symbols. This is a normal part of development: clarifying the principles that guide decisions.

Taking time to define these values helps a Leo make consistent choices. For example, if honesty ranks high for them, they will avoid hiding mistakes, even if it feels risky to admit them. If kindness is central, they might decide to lead in a more supportive, less rigid way. Over the years, living in line with values builds a strong identity.

This clarity can also provide comfort during setbacks. Even if a plan fails, a Leo who acted according to their values can stand tall, knowing they remained true to themselves. That sense of integrity can be more fulfilling than any short-term success. It also helps them earn genuine respect from others who see that the Leo does not sacrifice principles under pressure.

Learning from Role Models

Leos often find guidance by observing role models. These could be historical figures, community leaders, or even fictional characters who reflect traits they admire. A Leo might watch how a successful public figure handles criticism or how a beloved teacher treats struggling students with patience. Studying such examples can light up paths for personal growth.

Role models do not have to be famous. A family member who managed to balance raising children with a challenging job can be just as inspiring. The key is to look for qualities that resonate: resilience, empathy, courage, or creativity. By noting how these people navigate obstacles, a Leo can adapt those strategies in their own life.

That said, no role model is perfect. Recognizing that everyone has flaws can keep a Leo from feeling disillusioned if a favorite figure stumbles. Instead, they can take the positive lessons while acknowledging that humans are complex. This balanced view fosters realistic expectations and encourages a Leo to be patient with themselves as well.

Overcoming Negative Self-Talk

Despite their confident image, Leos can sometimes fall into negative thinking about themselves. This might happen after a public embarrassment, a setback, or if they feel overshadowed by someone else. Thoughts like "I should have done better" or "Maybe I am not as good as I thought" can creep in.

Personal growth involves noticing these thoughts without letting them control actions. A Leo might think, "I feel insecure right now, but that feeling does not define me." They can remind themselves of past successes or supportive words from trusted allies. They can also repeat affirmations that reflect their real strengths, such as "I am capable and ready to keep improving."

If negative self-talk becomes constant, it may help to speak with a counselor or confide in a mentor. Some negative beliefs are deep-rooted and might need an outside perspective to address effectively. Recognizing that it is okay to seek help is part of being a strong, self-aware person.

Harnessing Creativity for Growth

Because creativity is a strong part of many Leos' identities, they can lean on it to aid personal development. For instance, they might keep a personal scrapbook or sketch journal where they record moods or ideas. They could compose short songs about things they are learning. This creative process can make abstract concepts more tangible.

When facing a tough situation, they might brainstorm creative solutions instead of getting stuck in conventional thinking. The spark of imagination can turn a problem into a puzzle to be solved. Some Leos might stage small role-plays with friends to practice new communication methods. Others might illustrate their goals to visualize them better.

Creativity also helps them express emotions safely. If they are upset about a personal flaw or a slow rate of progress, painting or writing can let them explore those feelings. Doing so might reveal hidden insights that help them see the path forward. Over time, these creative outlets become trusted companions in the process of self-improvement.

Building Healthy Habits

Physical health and mental wellness support personal growth. A tired or unhealthy Leo might struggle to maintain enthusiasm, no matter how strong their will. Creating routines around exercise, good sleep, and balanced eating can enhance mood and energy levels, making it easier to pursue goals.

Healthy habits also provide structure. A Leo who goes for a morning walk each day has a consistent activity that clears their head before tackling challenges. Someone who sets a bedtime might find they wake up more focused. These small routines can stabilize life, freeing mental space for other types of growth.

It is not unusual for a Leo to prefer exciting new workouts or diets, but staying consistent might be the key. Rather than hopping from one trend to another, they can stick to a routine that truly fits their lifestyle and personal preferences. Over time, they will see the positive effects compound, boosting both body and spirit.

Accepting Help and Mentoring Others

Seeking a mentor and serving as a mentor can both drive personal growth. When Leos meet people who have walked a similar path, they can gain tips and avoid common mistakes. A wise mentor might gently challenge the Leo's perspective or suggest resources to expand their horizons. This guidance can speed up progress.

On the flip side, helping someone else grow can also teach a Leo a lot. If they tutor a younger student, lead a club, or guide a new coworker, they practice patience, empathy, and effective communication. They might spot old habits in the person they are helping, reminding them of how far they have come. This reflection can inspire them to continue improving.

Balancing these roles—learning from mentors while being a mentor—keeps Leos humble and engaged. They see they are part of a chain of knowledge and support. Nobody achieves everything alone, and passing on insights can be just as fulfilling as receiving them.

Being Patient with the Process

Leos, with their bold energy, might wish to speed through personal development. They could hope to master a skill or fix a flaw overnight. But real, deep change takes time. It requires trial, error, and steady practice. Rushing or expecting perfection too soon may leave them disappointed and tempted to quit.

Patience means forgiving themselves when they slip or revert to old habits. Maybe they wanted to be more diplomatic but found themselves snapping at a coworker. Instead of feeling defeated, they can treat it as a step in a longer progression. Over time, with steady effort, the moments of slipping grow less frequent.

They might also celebrate major shifts when they occur. If after months of effort, they handle a tense discussion with calm, they should acknowledge that milestone in a simple manner. It is a result of slow, deliberate work. This perspective helps them see growth as an ongoing path rather than a quick finish line.

CHAPTER 12: LEO'S LIKES AND DISLIKES

Every zodiac sign is often linked with certain tastes, interests, and aversions. For Leos, these preferences reflect their bold personality and affectionate nature. While not every Leo follows the same script, there are common themes that appear again and again. In this chapter, we will explore what many Leos tend to enjoy—such as certain activities, social settings, or styles—and also what they often find off-putting. By understanding these likes and dislikes, one can gain insight into how to connect with a Leo and recognize the factors that might spark tension or disinterest for them.

Preference for Warm and Welcoming Environments

Many Leos feel their best in settings that mirror their sunny spirits. They often enjoy places filled with light, bright colors, or a pleasant atmosphere. For instance, a Leo might love a living room decorated with bright tones or a restaurant that has an uplifting vibe. They may also feel drawn to warm climates, where the sunshine matches their inner glow.

Even in cooler places, Leos might bring touches of brightness. A Leo might decorate a workspace with cheerful items, like a vivid poster or a striking desk ornament. They appreciate spaces that make them feel at ease and energized. While not all Leos require constant sunshine, the presence of warmth—whether literal or symbolic—can boost their mood.

On the flip side, they might dislike drab or overly dull environments. A dark, cramped room with no personal flair might put a Leo off.

They prefer spots where they can move around freely, with a bit of visual excitement.

Enjoyment of Creative Outlets and Theatrical Fun

Leos are frequently attracted to creativity in many forms. They might relish watching theater, live music, or engaging in art projects. Anything that allows them to express imagination or see others doing the same tends to spark their interest. Activities like painting, dancing, acting, or singing can give them a natural high.

Even if they are not directly performing, Leos often enjoy being part of the audience. They might cheer the loudest at a play or applaud passionately at a concert. This enthusiasm often comes from their own fiery spirit, which resonates with creative energy.

They are less fond of experiences that feel monotonous or lack flair. For example, a repetitive task with no room for personal expression may bore them. They like to see some spark or room for originality. If an environment feels rigid and does not allow any creative spin, a Leo could quickly lose interest.

Social Gatherings and Personal Connections

Being around people can energize many Leos, especially if they have the chance to share stories, laughter, or ideas. A friendly gathering is often a favorite setting for them, whether it is a casual get-together with close friends or a large event. They thrive on interaction, enjoying the chance to chat and make others feel included.

Leos typically like gatherings where everyone has a role to play. They might offer to help organize activities or volunteer to direct the fun. Since they enjoy recognition, they often step up to lead or present. However, they can also flourish in smaller, more intimate groups, provided there is warmth and genuine sharing.

They might dislike gatherings that feel too quiet, tense, or cold. If the mood is gloomy and no one talks, a Leo might feel restless. They prefer an upbeat or at least welcoming vibe. They also dislike events where they sense fake niceness or forced politeness—sincerity matters to them.

Appreciation for Praise and Recognition

A common trait among Leos is valuing acknowledgment for their efforts or talents. This does not mean they are vain in a shallow way, but rather that they put their heart into what they do and enjoy knowing it has an impact. A simple compliment like, "I can see how much work you put into this," can lift a Leo's mood greatly.

They might also enjoy friendly competition when it is handled with mutual respect. Being recognized as a winner—or even as someone who performed well—can make a Leo feel motivated. However, if they sense that praise is fake or manipulative, they might react negatively. Genuine admiration is wonderful to them; flattery without sincerity is not.

On the dislike side, Leos may struggle when they feel completely ignored or taken for granted. If they put significant effort into a project or gesture and nobody notices, they can become disappointed or hurt. While they can learn to cope without constant applause, total disregard for their hard work can dampen their spirit.

Natural Draw to Leadership and Teamwork

Leos often enjoy stepping up to lead a group because it aligns with their confident nature. They may like tasks that let them organize people, provide direction, or guide discussions. In a team setting, they might volunteer as the spokesperson or the one who sums up ideas. This is not always about bossiness—many Leos feel happiest when they can coordinate efforts and help others succeed.

They also like group members who pull their weight. Since Leos can be quite driven, they might grow annoyed if someone consistently slacks off or undermines the team. They respect individuals who show effort, creativity, and fairness. A group that cooperates well, shares credit, and tackles goals with energy often delights them.

They can be frustrated in groups where they have no voice. If a Leo is forced into a background role with zero input, they might lose enthusiasm. They want a chance to contribute actively, whether as a leader or a valued teammate.

Love for Bold and Distinctive Styles

In personal style—be it fashion, art, or décor—Leos may enjoy being a bit daring. They might choose bright colors, unique patterns, or eye-catching accessories. If they can display their individuality through what they wear or how they decorate a room, they feel more alive.

This preference extends to the items they own. A Leo might select a phone case with a lively design or decorate a workspace with an eye-popping color scheme. They appreciate things that stand out. That does not always mean they dress in a flashy way, but they often pick at least one element that says, "Here I am."

A bland or overly minimal style might leave them feeling underwhelmed. While they can understand the appeal of simplicity, they often prefer a bit of flair. A home or outfit with zero personality may clash with their desire to see individuality in everyday life.

Fondness for Warm Colors and Rich Tones

Connected to the sun, many Leos have a natural liking for colors that reflect warmth and energy. Shades of gold, orange, yellow, and red can catch their eye. They might also appreciate deep tones like royal purple, which many link to royalty. Such hues match their sense of brightness and regal presence.

This can affect their choices in clothing, interior decoration, or even the art they display on walls. They might not wear these colors daily, but a bold pop of gold or a bright pattern might show up in their wardrobe. It is a reflection of their lively spirit.

On the other hand, dull or washed-out palettes may seem lifeless to them. While they can still enjoy neutral tones for balance, an environment that is entirely gray or beige could feel uninspiring. Leos generally prefer an element of vibrancy somewhere around them.

High-Energy Activities and Adventures

Leos often enjoy active pursuits, especially those that let them use their energy in a fun, social, or creative way. This might involve sports, dance lessons, outdoor hikes, or group fitness classes. They like to feel engaged and alive, seeing each activity as a chance to shine or connect with others.

They might also love traveling (going to new places), as it provides fresh experiences and challenges. The idea of exploring an exciting spot or taking part in a dynamic cultural event can appeal to them. They usually like to come back with stories to tell, which fits their dramatic side.

While they can relax at times, Leos might dislike a routine that feels too quiet or repetitive. Being stuck in the same dull tasks day in and day out can sap their spirit. They want at least occasional bursts of excitement or novelty to keep them feeling inspired.

Enjoying Comfort and Small Luxuries

Though they have a bold side, many Leos also have a soft spot for comfort. They might like plush sofas, soft blankets, or high-quality bedding. Items that provide a bit of indulgence, like a scented candle or a delicious treat, can brighten their day. It feels like a gentle way to pamper themselves or guests.

This fondness can extend to good food. A Leo might enjoy trying new flavors, going to a favorite restaurant, or hosting a meal at home with unique dishes. Sharing good times over a warm dinner table is often a treat for them, combining sociability and comfort.

However, they might be picky about low-quality or unappealing environments. A dusty, disorganized space could bother them. They want to feel that care has been put into creating a setting—whether it is a restaurant, a friend's home, or their own living area.

Dislike of Negativity or Dishonesty

While they understand that life is not always bright, Leos tend to steer clear of chronic negativity or deceptive behavior. If someone constantly complains without looking for solutions, a Leo might grow impatient. They believe in addressing problems actively rather than dwelling on them forever.

Dishonesty can also upset Leos deeply. Because they value openness, they feel disappointed if they catch someone in a lie. Trust is important to them. If they suspect manipulation, they are unlikely to stick around for long. That can apply to both personal relationships and professional settings.

This does not mean Leos expect eternal cheerfulness. They simply dislike when negativity becomes a habit or when people refuse to be genuine. If conflicts arise, they often prefer direct, honest talks to passive-aggressive comments or veiled hints.

Attraction to Drama

Leos can find excitement in dramatic stories, performances, or even spirited debates. That does not mean they want constant conflict, but they might enjoy a good story twist or a lively argument about a topic if it stays respectful. They appreciate strong emotions and expressive communication, as it resonates with their own fiery spirit.

In media, they may be drawn to movies or shows with big personalities, vibrant plots, and bold visuals. They might also like reading about dramatic events in history, relating to heroic figures or memorable leaders. These tales echo their inclination toward bravery and flair.

However, real-life drama that causes stress or chaos is a different story. A Leo might be excited by a lively discussion, but they usually do not want serious trouble or ongoing fights. They have their limits for drama in personal relationships, preferring when strong emotions lead to understanding rather than constant turmoil.

Enjoying Time Alone in Small Doses

While often seen as social and outgoing, Leos do appreciate occasional solitude. In those quiet moments, they can recharge, daydream, or plan their next move. They might read a book, work on an art piece, or simply unwind without the pressure of being "on" for others.

A short period of alone time can help them sort through ideas or ease any stress that comes from always being in the spotlight. It allows them to focus on personal tasks that require calm or reflection. Some Leos even find they can do their best creative work when they are by themselves.

That said, they might dislike being isolated for too long. Going days without social contact can make them feel restless or lonely. They usually prefer a balance between alone time and being around people, rather than extremes of constant party-going or total solitude.

Enjoyment of Storytelling and Humor

A sharp sense of humor is often a shared trait among Leos. They might be great at telling stories filled with funny details, capturing listeners' attention. This is not about being a stand-up comic necessarily; it is about using dramatic flair to make everyday events sound entertaining.

They like to see others laugh, and they usually respond well to jokes that match their energetic style. A comedic situation with over-the-top characters can spark their interest, and they might eagerly share comedic anecdotes from their own life.

On the dislike side, some Leos are turned off by humor that relies on cruelty or constant negativity. They enjoy jokes that are witty or playful, not those that target people's insecurities. They can dish out playful teasing, but they expect it to remain good-natured.

Admiration for Confidence in Others

Since Leos recognize confidence in themselves, they often respect it in other people as well. If someone walks into a room with self-assurance—not arrogance, but a calm sense of worth—they can quickly earn a Leo's admiration. Leos enjoy forming bonds with individuals who bring their own energy, share ideas, and stand firm in what they believe.

That said, they dislike show-offs who belittle others to look more important. The difference lies in attitude: a truly self-assured person does not have to put others down. A Leo who sees someone flaunting status while mocking those around them may be the first to call out that behavior or simply walk away.

They also do not respect false humility. If someone constantly acts helpless just for attention, a Leo might find it irritating. A healthy sense of self-worth tends to charm Leos more than either extreme: arrogance or fake meekness.

Attraction to Generosity and Kindness

Although they sometimes carry the image of wanting attention, most Leos genuinely appreciate kindness in themselves and in others. They respect people who share time, resources, or support with those who need it. Many Leos do the same, enjoying the sense of pride that comes from aiding a friend or improving their community.

They might dislike excessive stinginess or selfishness. If someone always takes but never gives, a Leo might gradually distance themselves. They believe in reciprocity—if they give warmth, they hope to see some warmth in return. It does not have to be the same kind of favor, but a simple gesture of gratitude goes a long way.

At social events, a Leo might be the person who offers to help set up or clean up after. They do not want to do it alone every time, but the team spirit appeals to them. People who show a similar willingness to pitch in can quickly become cherished companions.

Comfort with Being in the Spotlight

It is no secret that many Leos do not mind being the center of attention. They might willingly speak before a crowd, take charge of a group, or show off a new talent they have learned. They can have fun stepping into the limelight, especially when the environment is encouraging.

This interest in attention does not always mean they crave it every second. Leos simply do not shy away from the stage when it appears. In fact, they can feel restless if they never get a chance to showcase their strengths at all. They like to demonstrate what they have worked on or what excites them.

They are less fond of settings where nobody is allowed to shine. If rules or an atmosphere prevent anyone from showing personality, a Leo might see it as dull. They prefer a culture—whether at school, work, or in social circles—where achievements and unique traits are recognized.

Dislike of Disrespect or Undermining

Like anyone, Leos want to be treated respectfully. However, because of their strong sense of self, they can become especially irritated by disrespectful comments, backhanded remarks, or attempts to undermine their authority. They feel it as a direct challenge to their dignity.

This dislike can appear in both personal and professional contexts. A friend who constantly makes cutting jokes at their expense, or a colleague who dismisses their ideas in front of everyone, might trigger a Leo's anger or hurt. If the disrespect continues, the Leo might confront the issue or decide to remove themselves from the situation.

Yet, they respect constructive debate. If someone has a different opinion and shares it fairly, a Leo might be willing to listen. It is the tone and intent that matter. If they sense malice or hidden slights, that is when they become guarded or defensive.

Attraction to Loyalty and Reliability

Leos often see themselves as loyal friends who stand by loved ones through thick and thin. Consequently, they prize loyalty in return. If they know a friend is dependable, they feel safe sharing concerns or investing time in that friendship.

They tend to form long-lasting bonds with those who keep promises and support them in times of need. A loyal friend who shows up for big events or checks in during low moments is precious to them. Because they are protective, they might repay that loyalty by stepping in when a friend faces trouble.

Dishonesty or betrayal, however, can be a deal-breaker. If a Leo discovers that someone close to them has lied or broken trust, they can feel deeply wounded. It may take considerable effort to rebuild that relationship, if they choose to do so at all.

CHAPTER 13: HOW TO GET ALONG WITH A LEO

Getting along with a Leo can feel easier when you understand their nature. They are often described as warm, proud, and sometimes theatrical. Even though each Leo is unique, certain habits and values show up frequently. For people who want to form better friendships, family ties, or work partnerships with a Leo, it helps to know what inspires them and what might bother them. This chapter explains how to strengthen a connection with a Leo, from daily interactions to deeper bonds. By the end, you should have practical ways to appreciate a Leo's qualities, handle conflicts, and build lasting trust without stumbling over misunderstandings.

Show Honest Respect

One of the quickest ways to connect with a Leo is to offer respectful, genuine words or actions. Leos often invest a lot of energy in whatever they do, whether it is a creative project, a leadership role, or simply being there for friends. They typically appreciate when others notice that effort. A kind statement like, "You did an amazing job organizing this event" or "I really enjoy your ideas" can make them feel valued.

Still, they dislike hollow praise. They can usually sense when someone is saying nice things just to get something from them. If you want to offer positive feedback, be specific. For example, if a Leo friend prepared a meal, you could say, "The spices you chose made the dish taste really unique," rather than just "You're a great cook." This small detail shows that you truly saw their effort.

Respect also includes how you treat the Leo's opinions. Even if you disagree, take their views seriously. For instance, if you are in a group deciding on a plan, avoid laughing off their ideas too quickly. Instead, acknowledge their contribution: "That's interesting. Let's consider how we might include it." This approach often keeps a Leo open to other suggestions, and it shows you value their viewpoint.

Balance Attention with Personal Boundaries

Leos often enjoy standing out. They might talk passionately about their interests or want to lead in social situations. Giving them attention when they share a story or show a talent can strengthen your bond. Smiling, nodding, or asking questions indicates you are truly listening. These signals help them feel relaxed and appreciated.

However, every person has limits to how much attention they can give, and no Leo wants forced interest. You do not have to act fascinated by every detail if it feels unnatural. Just be honest but polite. If a Leo is talking about something that does not interest you, you can still listen kindly. You might respond with, "I appreciate your excitement, though I'm not very familiar with this topic. Can you tell me more about why you like it?" That way, you respect their enthusiasm without pretending you share it fully.

Also, recognize that Leos need space, too. While they do enjoy attention, many Leos value alone time when they want to recharge or work on personal tasks. If a Leo friend seems to be in a quieter mood, do not force them to perform or lead. Let them step back if they wish. By respecting both their bright side and their quieter moments, you show deeper understanding.

Offer Support When They Feel Insecure

Leos often appear confident. They might be the ones to speak up first, plan group activities, or share big dreams. However, beneath that confidence, they can also feel doubts. If something goes wrong—like a project fails or a friend ignores them—Leos might take it personally. They might wonder if they are not as talented or liked as they thought.

When you notice a Leo feeling down, gently reassure them. You might say something like, "I know you put a lot into this. One setback doesn't erase all the good you've done." Encourage them to see setbacks as learning points instead of proof that they are lacking. Leos respond well to genuine kindness. Telling them their strengths and reminding them of past victories can lift their spirits, as long as it is sincere.

Also, try not to brush off their worries by saying, "You shouldn't feel that way," because that might make them feel overlooked. Instead, acknowledge their feelings with a simple statement, such as, "I can see why this is bothering you. It's understandable." Showing empathy often helps a Leo feel safe enough to bounce back, which they usually do.

Give Them a Chance to Shine in Groups

Whether at school, work, or among friends, many Leos flourish when given a role that matches their natural confidence. They might enjoy presenting ideas, leading a discussion, or heading a creative venture. If you are in a position to delegate tasks, consider offering a Leo a role where they can use their enthusiasm and boldness. They often do well in tasks that involve motivating others, public speaking, or planning special events.

That said, be mindful of balancing the group's needs. A Leo can be a strong motivator, but if they overshadow quieter teammates, it can lead to tension. A good approach is to talk to the Leo privately and say, "You have great leadership skills. I also want to make sure others share their ideas. Can you help me encourage them?" This request turns their leadership into a positive force that benefits everyone.

Similarly, if you are not the one assigning roles, you can still speak up for a Leo who is well-suited to a leadership position. Something like, "I think Alex (the Leo) has strong organizational skills; maybe they could guide this part of the project," can help them step into a spot where they excel.

Set Clear Communication

Leos appreciate directness. If something is bothering you, it is often better to address it calmly rather than letting tension build. For example, if you feel a Leo friend is dominating every conversation, you might say, "I love hearing your stories, but I also want to share something about my day. Can we find some balance?" Using a friendly tone can prevent them from feeling attacked.

Likewise, if a Leo upsets you, telling them straightforwardly is more effective than dropping hints. They might not pick up on subtle signals. They will usually respond better to, "It hurts me when you ignore my input in group decisions," rather than coded remarks like, "Sure, go ahead with your usual way." A direct statement can clear the air faster.

However, keep your tone respectful. If a Leo senses contempt, they may become defensive. Statements like, "You always have to be the center of attention!" can spark an argument. Instead, focus on how the behavior affects you: "I sometimes feel ignored when you speak over me." This approach invites understanding rather than causing a fight.

Encourage Their Creativity

Many Leos are drawn to creative pursuits. They might enjoy painting, singing, writing, designing, or any other activity that lets them explore ideas. If you see a Leo working on a creative project, show genuine interest. Ask about their process, the inspiration behind it, or what they hope to achieve. Encouraging questions like, "Where did you get that color idea?" or "What do you want people to feel when they see your artwork?" show real curiosity.

If you have the means, you can offer small gestures to support their creativity. For instance, sharing art supplies you no longer need, recommending a new technique you discovered, or inviting them to an art event can show you respect their passions. In group settings, you might suggest, "Let's ask Jordan (the Leo) for design ideas. They have a knack for making things look exciting." This highlights their strengths and can boost their confidence.

Avoid dismissing their creative ideas just because they seem grand or unusual. Leos often think big, and even if you do not share their vision, acknowledging their enthusiasm is courteous. You can politely express any concerns—like time or cost limitations—while still praising the originality behind their ideas.

Respect Their Sense of Pride

Leos take pride in who they are and what they accomplish. Critiques or jokes that belittle them in front of others can do real harm to your relationship. When you need to offer suggestions for improvement, do it in private, with a tone that shows you have their best interests at heart. For instance, "I noticed you seemed stressed leading that meeting. Maybe we can plan next time together so it's smoother?" frames the feedback as caring collaboration.

If a Leo feels publicly embarrassed or humiliated, it can be tough for them to let go. Try to avoid scolding them or calling out mistakes in front of an audience. One-on-one conversations work better. Most Leos respond better to calm explanations and mutual respect than to being shamed.

Also, if you see others mocking a Leo in an unkind way, stepping in gently might improve the bond you share. You could redirect the topic or say something like, "Let's keep it respectful, please." They will likely remember your support, which can deepen trust.

Be Open to Their Big Plans

It is not unusual for a Leo to share grand dreams or talk about ambitious goals. They might want to start a company, direct a film, or make a significant community project. While some people might dismiss these ideas as unrealistic, keep in mind that Leos often thrive on big visions. Listening and giving them space to brainstorm can strengthen your connection.

That does not mean you have to be a "yes-person." If you see potential issues, you can voice them kindly. "It sounds like a great plan, but have you considered the budget?" is less dismissive than, "That will never work." Focus on solutions and how they might overcome hurdles. A Leo who senses your belief in their abilities—along with constructive hints—may be more motivated to refine their plan.

If they run into obstacles with their big idea, encourage them to see it as part of the path to success. Remind them that adjusting a plan is not the same as giving up. By helping them stay grounded yet optimistic, you become a trusted ally in their pursuit of something they find meaningful.

Accept Their Generous Gestures

Leos can be quite generous. They might host gatherings, pay for a friend's meal, or give thoughtful gifts. Some do it because they enjoy making others smile, while others feel it is part of their role as a caring person. If you sense a Leo's generosity is genuine, you can accept it gratefully. A sincere "Thank you, that means a lot" can show that you appreciate their kindness.

Sometimes, people refuse such gestures because they feel uncomfortable. But if you consistently reject a Leo's attempts to be generous, they might interpret it as you not trusting them or not valuing their friendship. Instead, find small, meaningful ways to reciprocate. You do not have to match them exactly, but writing a note of thanks, or giving them something personal (like a homemade treat) later on, can show you are not just taking without giving back in your own way.

However, if you ever feel that a Leo's generosity is too much or has strings attached, calmly address it. A gentle statement like, "I truly appreciate your gift, but I worry it's more than I can accept comfortably," might help them see your perspective. Most Leos do not want you to feel uneasy, so honest communication can resolve misunderstandings.

Stay True to Yourself

While trying to get along with a Leo, do not forget your own identity. Leos often respect people who hold to their own values rather than simply going along with everything. If a Leo friend suggests an activity you do not enjoy, it is okay to say politely, "That's not my favorite, but I'm open to trying something else." They may appreciate your honesty more than you pretending to like something you do not.

At the same time, remain open-minded to new experiences a Leo might introduce. They often have a flair for interesting adventures. Perhaps they invite you to an art exhibit or plan a spontaneous trip somewhere close by. Even if it is new territory for you, consider giving it a try—you might discover something exciting. If you genuinely do not enjoy it, you can still say, "Thanks for taking me along. It's interesting to see what you like, even though it might not be fully my style."

Remember that healthy friendships and relationships grow best when both parties respect each other's individuality. By showing that you have your own preferences while still celebrating the Leo's passions, you create a balanced dynamic where neither person feels forced to compromise too much.

Handle Disagreements Calmly

Arguments are normal in any relationship, and with a Leo, differences might arise because of their passionate nature. They might stand firm on their viewpoints, so if you disagree, aim for calm, clear communication. Try statements like, "I see your side. Here's my view," or "I get why you feel that way, but I have a different perspective."

Avoid attacking their character. If you focus on calling them "bossy" or "selfish," the discussion can become an emotional standoff. Instead, comment on specific behaviors. For example, "When you make decisions without asking me, I feel overlooked," is about an action rather than an insult.

Also, try to resolve matters sooner rather than later. Letting silent resentment grow can harm trust. If a Leo sees you calmly bringing up concerns, they might feel safe admitting their own frustrations. That openness can lead to deeper mutual understanding, even if you do not fully agree on every point.

Recognize Their Emotional Swings

Leos can have mood swings, like anyone else, though their highs and lows might be more visible. When they are excited, they can fill a room with joy. When they are upset, they might express it strongly. If you notice a sudden change in their mood, do not panic—often, they just need time to process.

Sometimes a Leo might retreat if they feel hurt, which can seem out of character. If you sense they are pulling away, gently ask if they need to talk. If they decline, respect their boundary but leave the door open: "I'm here whenever you're ready, okay?" This approach tells them you care without forcing them to share before they are ready.

When they come out of a low moment, try not to hold their gloom against them. If they snapped at you or were unusually distant, and they apologize, accept it if you can. People with strong emotional currents often need that release, and a caring response can help restore closeness. Of course, if you feel the outbursts are too frequent or harmful, setting healthy boundaries is important. Leos are often willing to listen if you explain how their actions affect you.

Acknowledge Their Loyal Streak

Leos can be incredibly loyal to those they care about. If you ever need support—maybe you are dealing with a personal worry or a bigger life challenge—do not be afraid to approach your Leo friend or relative. Many of them jump at the chance to defend or help the people they love. By trusting them enough to confide, you show them that you value their reliability.

When they do stand by you, show appreciation. "I'm really thankful you had my back during that argument," or "Your help made a big difference when I was feeling down," can confirm the bond. This kind of direct gratitude helps them see that their loyalty is noticed. In turn, they will likely continue offering support in future challenges.

Also, if you make a promise to a Leo, keep it. They hold loyalty in high regard and can feel especially hurt by broken promises. If something happens and you cannot keep your word, explain the reason honestly and offer to make it up to them if possible.

Give Them Constructive Outlets for Their Energy

Leos can possess a lot of energy, sometimes needing an outlet to burn it off. This might take the shape of group sports, creative sessions, or lively social outings. If you sense a Leo is restless, suggest an activity that matches their energy, like an impromptu party with board games, a small backyard sports match, or a quick trip to a place nearby for fresh air.

In more formal settings, like a classroom or workplace, encourage them to channel their drive into meaningful tasks. For instance, if they are bored, you might say, "We could really use someone to oversee the final presentation. You have the enthusiasm for it." This helps them find a purposeful way to use their energy instead of being idle or disruptive.

On the other hand, if a Leo's energy is overwhelming, calmly communicate the need for a more relaxed pace. "I appreciate your excitement, but I need a quieter approach right now. Maybe we can pick a calmer activity?" Many Leos are flexible if they see you are sincere and not just rejecting them outright.

Avoid Manipulative Behavior

Trying to play mind games with a Leo is often a bad idea. They tend to spot dishonest tactics, and it can break trust quickly. If you want something from a Leo, be direct. For example, if you need their help with a school assignment or a work project, say, "I would really appreciate your assistance. Could you lend me your skills here?" rather than using flattery just to manipulate them.

Leos might also walk away from relationships where they sense they are constantly used. They want genuine bonds, not ones based on trickery or hidden motives. If you remain open, honest, and fair, you are more likely to keep a Leo's respect and friendship.

Likewise, do not encourage them to manipulate you. If you sense they are pushing you to do something that feels uncomfortable, calmly but firmly state your boundary. Most Leos, when treated with clarity, will back down and respect your choice if they see your refusal is firm yet polite.

Enjoy Shared Humor and Light Moments

A good laugh can bring you closer to a Leo. Many of them have a playful sense of humor and like teasing banter—as long as it is not mean-spirited. You can crack inside jokes or recall funny memories together. Just be careful about jokes that touch on their pride. Light teasing can be fun, but if it seems like you are undermining them in a hurtful way, it might backfire.

Sharing silly experiences, like watching a comedic movie together or playing fun group games, can strengthen your connection. Leos often light up during these relaxed, cheerful times. If they make a pun or do a funny impression, laugh if you find it genuinely amusing. That reaction encourages their playful side without forcing anything.

You can also pay attention to what kind of humor they prefer. Some Leos love witty wordplay, while others enjoy slapstick comedy. Tuning in to these details shows you are paying attention to their likes, which can lead to more enjoyable moments together.

Help Them Manage Stress

Leos can juggle many tasks, sometimes pushing themselves too hard because they do not want to appear weak or unprepared. If you notice a Leo friend or coworker looking overwhelmed, you might offer, "Need a hand with anything?" or "I can take care of this small piece if it helps." Simple gestures can ease their load without implying they cannot handle the core tasks.

If a Leo seems on the brink of burnout, gentle reminders to rest can help. "You've been working a lot lately—maybe it's time for a short break?" can show them that you notice their well-being. Some Leos might initially resist, saying they are fine. Do not nag, but continue to show you care if they look tired. Over time, they may realize you have their interests at heart and accept assistance.

Offering stress relief activities—like a casual walk, a calm chat, or a mild exercise class—might also help them reset. The key is to propose without insisting. A statement like, "It might be nice to clear our heads. Want to come with me for a short walk?" can be more appealing than commanding them, "You need to rest right now."

CHAPTER 14: LEO AND COMMUNICATION

Communication styles can differ greatly from one zodiac sign to another. In the case of Leo, the way they speak and listen can be shaped by their warm, bold spirit. They often share ideas with flair, whether in casual chats or official settings. But communication is not just about talking—it also involves listening, reading subtle cues, and managing conflicts. By learning how Leo typically expresses themselves, as well as what helps them understand others, you can have more open and positive interactions with them. In this chapter, we will examine how Leo communicates in different contexts, from friendly talks to serious debates, and how to avoid misunderstandings that can arise when a person with such a strong personality shares thoughts and feelings.

Direct Yet Expressive Speech

Many Leos are known for speaking with confidence. Even if they are discussing everyday matters, their tone can be lively, drawing attention. They might use larger gestures or emphasize key points to keep listeners engaged. When excited, they may talk quickly, layering details and personal feelings into what could otherwise be a simple story.

This expressive style can make a conversation with a Leo quite fun. If you show interest—like nodding, smiling, and asking follow-up questions—they will feel encouraged to share more. On the other hand, if you remain silent and stone-faced, they might feel you are bored or dismissive. A little feedback goes a long way in helping them feel heard.

At times, a Leo's direct manner might sound blunt. They might state opinions such as, "This approach isn't working," without sugarcoating. If you sense they are being too straightforward, you can respond by saying something like, "I understand what you mean, but could you explain your reasoning more calmly?" or "I hear you, but let's slow down and talk through each point." This can guide them toward a calmer mode of expression without shutting them down.

Strong Eye Contact and Body Language

Because Leos are often comfortable with attention, they might look you in the eye while talking. They may also use hand movements or change the pitch of their voice to highlight specific ideas. Observing these clues can give you insight into their emotions. If a Leo's eyes light up and their hands start moving, it usually means they are very passionate about the topic.

Similarly, if a Leo's posture suddenly droops or they avoid eye contact, it might suggest disappointment or hurt. When that happens, a gentle prompt like, "You seem a bit off. Want to talk about it?" can let them know you care. They might appreciate that you noticed the shift.

Leos also appreciate when you engage with your own body language. Face them directly if possible, nod or smile when appropriate, and avoid distractions like checking your phone too often. Simple gestures like these convey that you value their words.

Listening Gaps and Patience

Though many Leos enjoy talking, they also respond well to good listening skills in others. If you interrupt them too often or let your mind wander, they may notice quickly. In turn, they may feel unappreciated. Giving a Leo enough space to finish their thoughts before chiming in helps them feel respected.

On the other hand, some Leos can become so enthusiastic that they forget to pause and let others speak. If you find yourself struggling to join the conversation, gently say something like, "I'd love to add a thought here—can I jump in?" Usually, a Leo who respects you will realize they need to let you share as well.

Patience can be key. If a Leo is on a roll with a story, cutting them off abruptly might upset them. Try waiting for a natural break in their speech. If none appears, politely interject with, "That sounds fascinating—do you mind if I respond to one point?" or "I want to share something related before we move on." This method respects their flow while also ensuring you get a turn.

Emotional Expressions in Communication

Leos may openly express how they feel, whether it is joy, frustration, pride, or sadness. When they are happy, you might hear it in the excitement of their voice. When they are upset, it can come out in strong words or a change in tone. This openness helps others sense what is on their mind, but it can also lead to heated moments if the emotion is negative.

If a Leo becomes emotional while talking—like raising their voice in anger—try to remain calm. You can say, "I want to understand what's bothering you, but it's hard when things are this tense. Can we slow down and talk it through?" By focusing on the goal of understanding rather than arguing, you can help redirect the discussion.

Similarly, if a Leo is bursting with excitement over good news, join their celebration if you can. Offer supportive words and share in their enthusiasm. "That's fantastic! Tell me more about how you did it," can make them feel you are genuinely happy for them. This can build a deeper sense of connection.

Written and Digital Communication

Not all interaction with a Leo happens face-to-face. Texts, emails, and social media chats can also be important. You might notice that some Leos prefer a lively style in writing, using exclamation points or creative emojis. Their messages could be longer, too, since they like to give details.

When writing to a Leo, adding a friendly tone can help. Instead of a dull message like, "Meeting is at 2 PM," you might say, "Hey, looking forward to brainstorming together at 2 PM!"—assuming you have that level of closeness. If it is a work-related email, you can maintain respect while still sounding upbeat.

Keep an eye out for misread cues. Without hearing voice tones, a text can seem sharper or colder than intended. If a Leo's response sounds abrupt, consider that they might just be busy or focusing on something else. You can calmly ask for clarity: "Is everything okay? Your message felt a bit short—just checking in." This approach can prevent small misunderstandings from growing.

Handling Criticism and Conflict

When they receive criticism, Leos might react strongly at first. They often take pride in their work and can feel stung if someone points out flaws or mistakes. If you must give a Leo constructive feedback, it helps to choose your words carefully. Aim for a tone that shows you want them to succeed, such as, "I see a lot of promise here. Maybe adjusting this section would make it even better."

This approach frames the critique as a route to improvement rather than a negative judgment. You might say something like, "You have a great speaking presence. If you slow down just a bit, people will catch every word." By acknowledging their strengths first, you make it easier for them to hear the suggestion.

If a conflict arises, and a Leo seems defensive, try not to mirror their intensity. Instead, maintain a calm but firm stance. "I understand this is important to you. Here's what I'm feeling…" can help them see your side without feeling attacked. Then, invite them to share their perspective. Active listening at this stage shows you respect their viewpoint, even if you disagree on details.

Using Clear Words for Assurance

Leos can get worried about losing standing in a relationship or group. If you sense they feel overlooked, direct reassurance can soothe them. Phrases like, "Your input really helped me," "I'm so glad you're part of this project," or "You make a big difference here" confirm their worth. Be honest—do not say it if you do not mean it, but if you do, it can strengthen trust.

When a Leo friend or partner is down, sometimes it is enough to say, "I appreciate having you in my life," or "Thank you for always bringing good energy." They tend to respond well to heartfelt statements. If you combine kind words with a supportive action—like helping them with a small task or showing up for an event that matters to them—it speaks even more loudly.

However, watch out for overdoing reassurance if you are not comfortable. Too many compliments might sound forced. Genuine, well-timed remarks are often more powerful than an avalanche of praise. A single, heartfelt line can mean more to a Leo than multiple casual statements that lack real substance.

Encouraging Them to Listen Actively

Leos can sometimes get carried away talking about their achievements or plans. If you want them to hear your side, you may have to gently guide them toward active listening. You could say, "I appreciate hearing your experiences. Could we pause so I can share mine too?" or "That's really interesting. I'd also like to tell you what happened to me last week."

By framing it as a request rather than a complaint, you are more likely to get a positive response. Most Leos do want to be fair, but they might forget if their excitement is high. Once you have the floor, keep your points clear and share them in a calm manner. They will usually realize they need to give you the same respect they desire.

If a Leo consistently struggles to listen, consider a private chat. You might say, "I love talking with you, but I sometimes feel like you do not hear me out. Could we try balancing our time when we chat?" If they see it as a genuine path to a better relationship, they may adjust their habits.

Flexibility in Discussing Plans

Leos, with their strong sense of direction, might present an idea as if it is the final answer. In group discussions, they could say, "Let's do it my way," expecting others to follow. If you have a different plan, do not hesitate to suggest it politely: "That sounds good, but here's another possibility we might consider."

When both sides show willingness to adapt, solutions emerge more easily. If the Leo's proposal truly is best, you can go with it while still adding small improvements. If your idea is better, you can explain the benefits clearly. Show them how it aligns with the overall goals.

A Leo who sees the advantages might step back and say, "Okay, let's try your approach," especially if you frame it as a team victory.

Stay calm if they sound pushy. They might not realize they are coming across that way. A gentle reminder—"We want everyone's ideas on the table before deciding"—can refocus the chat on group input. Often, the Leo will appreciate that you are trying to include everyone rather than going against them.

Tone and Word Choice Matter

Because Leos can be sensitive to how things are said, pay attention to tone. Even a short phrase like "What do you want?" can sound hostile if spoken harshly. Changing it to "What would you like to do?" in a friendlier tone can make all the difference. The words themselves and how they are delivered carry emotional weight for a Leo.

They also tend to notice sarcasm or insincerity. If you feel tense about an issue, try to be straightforward rather than using mocking remarks. Sarcastic statements can hurt the Leo's feelings more than you might expect. They may take them as real attacks rather than playful comments, especially if they are already stressed.

When a Leo uses a sharp tone with you, it is okay to mention how it makes you feel. "I want to talk this through, but your words seem harsh right now, and I'm feeling uneasy." This can help them realize they are coming off more aggressively than intended. Once they see how it affects you, many Leos will adjust their approach if they value the relationship.

Adaptation in Serious Dialogues

Not every conversation is light and fun. If you need to address a major topic—like relationship rules, work responsibilities, or money concerns—approach a Leo with clarity. Start by stating the main reason: "I want to talk about how we share finances," or "We need to discuss boundaries in our relationship."

Then, invite their view: "How do you feel about it?" Let them express themselves fully before offering your points. If they get dramatic, try to keep calm and encourage them to slow down: "I hear your passion, but I want to be sure we cover all details carefully." Summaries can also help: "So you are saying you feel worried about overspending, is that correct?" It shows you are truly listening.

Once each side has talked, aim for a compromise or a clear action plan. "You handle groceries, and I'll cover utilities—does that sound fair?" or "We agree to set aside time every week to check in on how things are going?" A well-structured approach keeps big issues from turning into shouting matches or confusion.

Recognizing Their Communication Triggers

Leos may have certain triggers that spark strong reactions. Common ones include feeling dismissed, having their work overlooked, or being publicly criticized. Notice these patterns if you interact with a Leo often. For example, if you see them tense up when someone interrupts them mid-sentence, that is a clue to let them finish next time.

If you accidentally hit one of these triggers, step back and apologize if needed. "I'm sorry I cut you off—I realize you were making an important point," can cool the tension. Then let them continue or clarify. By doing so, you show you respect their communication needs.

Over time, understanding these triggers can keep talks smoother. You can present feedback in a gentle way or pick a private moment instead of calling them out in front of others. The aim is not to tiptoe around them but to use empathy in how you phrase things.

Avoiding Excessive Flattery

While Leos like compliments, too much praise can seem suspicious. If every word out of your mouth is, "You're the best! Everything you do is perfect!" they might grow skeptical. It can feel like you are trying to manipulate them, or that your words lack honesty.

Balance is key. Recognize genuine achievements and qualities you admire, but do not force compliments for no reason. You can also share constructive feedback or your own perspective once in a while, which shows that you are not just nodding to everything they say. This approach helps a Leo see you as a real person with your own views, rather than someone who only praises them.

Leos usually prefer a relationship that has genuine depth over one built on forced niceties. In fact, they may respect you more if they see you have your own opinions and are not afraid to express them kindly.

Group Communication and Public Speaking

If you and a Leo are addressing a crowd—maybe in a school presentation or a workplace meeting—Leos often do well as speakers. They might volunteer to be the main voice. If you are both comfortable with that, let them handle the spotlight. However, plan together so they know when to pass the microphone (literally or figuratively) to you or others.

When giving group instructions, a Leo might sound commanding. This can be helpful if the group needs direction but can alienate people who want their voices heard. You can help by stepping in with short lines like, "That's a great starting plan. Let's also hear ideas from the rest of the team." If the Leo sees you as an ally, they will likely support this approach.

If you are the one leading, keep the Leo engaged by giving them a role that matches their strengths. For instance, ask them to handle introductions or summarize the group's final conclusions. This inclusion can satisfy their desire to contribute meaningfully while letting you remain in charge of the broader conversation.

Social Media and Public Image

Some Leos care a lot about how they appear online. They may carefully choose the photos they post or the words they use in social media updates. This does not mean they are "fake." Rather, they often see social media as an extension of their real self, where they can express confidence or creativity.

If you interact with a Leo on social platforms, respectful engagement—like leaving a supportive comment or responding to their stories—can make them smile. Avoid rude or mocking remarks in public threads, as they may take it more personally than you intend. If you have a criticism, consider sending it via a private message or talking face-to-face.

When you share photos or details that include a Leo friend, ask their permission first if you suspect they might be sensitive about how they are presented. A simple "Do you mind if I post this picture of us?" or "Are you okay with me tagging you?" shows courtesy. Most Leos appreciate the thoughtfulness and might say yes quickly. If they say no, respect that choice to maintain a positive atmosphere.

Learning from Their Assertiveness

Leos can show you ways to be more confident in your own communication. Notice how they speak up for themselves or present big ideas without shame. You could learn that it is okay to propose your dream project at work or share your strong opinions in a debate. The key is to do it with self-belief rather than fear of what others might think.

If you admire this part of their character, you can ask them for pointers. "You speak so firmly in team meetings—how do you calm your nerves?" They might have tips on preparing notes, practicing in front of a mirror, or reminding themselves they have value. This can encourage you to find your own assertive side while preserving your personal style.

That said, remain authentic. You do not need to copy a Leo's dramatic flair exactly. Instead, let their self-assured approach inspire you to be more open and true to yourself in communication. A mix of your unique voice and a bit more boldness could help you succeed in many areas of life.

Knowing When to Lighten the Mood

If a Leo is feeling tense, humor or a playful comment might diffuse the stress—provided it is well-timed. For example, if they are upset about a minor setback, you could gently remind them of a past funny memory: "Remember the time you tried to fix the old TV and it started working out of nowhere? You have the magic touch, so I'm sure you'll figure this out too!"

However, be cautious about cracking jokes if the topic is very serious. If the Leo is dealing with a genuine crisis, a joke could come across as insensitive. Gauge the situation carefully. If their upset is mild, a bit of lightheartedness can help them see a bright side. If it is major, offer comfort or solutions rather than jokes.

When a Leo tries to lighten your mood, they might tell a dramatic story or share an amusing anecdote. Show appreciation if it cheers you up. "You always know how to make me laugh. Thanks." This response supports their attempt and shows you are not brushing off their efforts.

Encouraging Open-Ended Questions

Leos may respond well to questions that let them expand on their thoughts. Instead of "Did you like the movie?" you could ask, "What did you think about the storyline or the characters?" Such open-ended questions invite them to dive deeper into their viewpoints, giving them a chance to display that expressive side they love.

You can also ask about their goals, inspirations, or personal challenges. "What made you choose that design style?" or "How do you stay motivated when facing obstacles?" can spark interesting conversations where the Leo reveals more about their inner world. In turn, you learn what drives them and can better support their future plans.

However, if they seem reluctant to share certain details, respect their boundary. Not every Leo wants to talk about personal topics. Some may prefer to keep certain matters private until they trust you more. Being patient and understanding can lay a foundation for deeper communication later.

Observing Nonverbal Agreements

In conversation, Leos might rely on small signs to confirm agreement. They could nod firmly or use a quick phrase like "Exactly!" or "Right!" to show they are on board. If you are looking for a more formal answer—like an absolute yes or no—politely clarify: "Just to confirm, are we both agreeing on this plan?" That step ensures you are not assuming their nod means something more concrete than it does.

Similarly, they may check your response in subtle ways. If you respond with a half-smile, they could ask, "Are you okay with that?" or "You seem unsure." Recognize that they might be seeking clarity to avoid confusion later. It is often best to respond plainly if you are uncertain: "I'm not fully sure yet, but I'll let you know once I think it through."

When boundaries are at stake, do not rely on hints. If you need a Leo to respect a specific limit, say so directly: "I need you not to share this information with anyone," or "I'm not comfortable discussing that topic." Clear statements can prevent misunderstandings that might otherwise cause tension.

Building a Lasting Communication Style

In the end, communicating well with a Leo often means blending honesty, warmth, and a bit of patience. By letting them speak with passion, offering sincere feedback, and setting fair boundaries, you create an environment where both sides can express themselves freely. Leos usually admire people who show genuine interest in their ideas while also having unique thoughts of their own.

Keep in mind that each Leo is still an individual. Some may be more introverted, while others lean extra strongly into their sociable nature. Tailoring your approach to the specific Leo in your life is always wise. Watch how they respond, ask for their thoughts on how to communicate better, and adapt as you learn more about them.

CHAPTER 15: LEO'S CONNECTION TO CONFIDENCE

Confidence is often considered one of Leo's strongest traits. Many people describe Leos as bold and self-assured, comfortable leading the pack or standing in the spotlight. Yet, confidence has many layers. It can rise and fall depending on life events, relationships, or self-perception. In this chapter, we will explore why confidence tends to be so linked with Leo, how it can show up in different situations, and the ways Leos can keep it balanced and healthy. We will also look at what happens when a Leo's confidence wavers, and how they can restore it in a constructive way.

Why Confidence Is Tied to Leo

Leos are symbolized by the lion, which is often portrayed as a regal creature unafraid to roam proudly. Over centuries, astrology has associated Leos with qualities like bravery, leadership, and shining energy. This zodiac sign is also linked to the sun, seen as a bright force that brings warmth and life. Because of these associations, many people believe that Leos naturally show courage and a willingness to step forward.

In practical life, many Leos do enjoy taking on roles that let them express themselves. They might speak up in class, volunteer to lead a project at work, or plan group outings among friends. This willingness to act can look like confidence to those around them. And often, it is a real sense of inner assurance—they believe in their ability to learn and succeed.

At the same time, not all Leos display this in the same manner. Some may appear quieter, but still hold a strong sense of self-worth inside. Others might show their confidence in creative pursuits, like painting or performing music. The key idea is that Leos typically feel a push to share their talents and ideas with others. That drive can look like confidence, especially when matched with an outgoing personality.

Different Styles of Leo Confidence

While the label "confident" gets attached to many Leos, there is more than one style of confidence. Here are a few ways it can appear:

Outgoing and Bold: This is the classic image people often have of a Leo—someone who speaks with a clear voice, laughs heartily, and does not hesitate to be seen. They might take charge in group projects, stand at the front of a class, or show a natural flair in performances.

Calm and Self-Possessed: Some Leos do not speak loudly or wave their arms around. Instead, they project a quiet firmness. They might sit in a group discussion, listening carefully, and then offer a statement that carries weight. Their confidence appears in measured actions rather than loud announcements.

Creative and Expressive: Another form of Leo confidence can appear in artistic work. A Leo might put on an art show, share original writing, or design something eye-catching. Their confidence is in showing their personal style, even if they do not crave public speaking.

Supportive Leader: Leos with a nurturing streak may channel confidence into guiding or helping others. They are self-assured enough to stand by someone, give advice, or offer encouragement in a crisis. Their sense of self often allows them to be strong when others feel weak.

In all these styles, Leos rely on a belief in their capabilities or their right to be heard. Even if they have doubts, they usually find a spark within that says, "I can face this." Still, each person's upbringing, environment, and life experiences affect how they show that spark.

Early Roots of Leo Confidence

Childhood can play a major role in shaping how a Leo's confidence unfolds. If a young Leo grows up in a supportive family that applauds their efforts—like praising them for trying a new skill—they may learn that sharing talents brings good feedback. They could become more eager to speak up or try new activities as they get older.

On the other hand, a Leo child who faces constant criticism or neglect might develop hidden insecurities. They might long to show their abilities but worry about being shut down. In some cases, they might overcompensate by acting overly proud or by seeking lots of attention. Alternatively, they might hide their gifts to avoid further negative responses. Over time, they could learn to rebuild confidence through other supportive relationships, mentors, or personal successes.

School environments matter too. A Leo who excels in a subject might enjoy presenting projects or volunteering answers, while one who struggles in a certain area might become reluctant to participate. Teachers who recognize a Leo's natural drive for expression and offer constructive feedback can help that student become more self-assured. The same goes for peers: supportive friends encourage a Leo to keep sharing talents, while constant teasing can make them withdraw or act out in overly dramatic ways.

Confidence vs. Arrogance

Sometimes, outsiders might see a Leo's confidence as arrogance. They might think, "That person always talks about themselves," or "They never ask about others." While it can happen that a Leo goes too far and becomes self-centered, in many cases the difference is in the Leo's motive. A healthy confidence often appears as enthusiasm or readiness to lead, not as a put-down to others.

When does confidence tip into arrogance? Usually when the Leo (or anyone) starts to believe they are above others or that only their ideas matter. Instead of saying, "I have a great idea—let's explore it," arrogance might say, "My idea is the only one that counts, so everyone else should be quiet." That attitude often closes off collaboration.

Self-assured Leos with healthy boundaries try to maintain openness to other perspectives. They might say, "I believe in my plan, but let's see if your approach can fit in too." Meanwhile, an arrogant person might dismiss others immediately. By watching how a Leo (or any sign) treats differing opinions, you can often tell if their confidence is genuine or slipping into self-importance.

Confidence in Social Circles

Leos often enjoy social gatherings, partly because it gives them a chance to shine. They might talk animatedly about their interests, lead group games, or break the ice when new people join. Their sense of confidence can help them make new friends easily. They do not shy away from introducing themselves or starting a conversation.

At the same time, this visible self-assurance can prompt some onlookers to label a Leo as "too much." If a group is more reserved, the Leo might seem too loud or attention-seeking. This can cause friction. However, a self-aware Leo will usually sense the group's tone and adjust, toning down their style if they see others are uncomfortable with big energy.

Among close friends, a confident Leo might become a pillar of support. Because they believe in their capacity to handle problems, they can encourage a friend through difficulties. They might say, "We can solve this," with real conviction. Their confidence can spread, giving the friend a bit more hope. A well-adjusted Leo friend can become a natural motivator in social circles.

Career and Work Situations

In a workplace, a Leo's confidence often shows up in leadership or in roles that require initiative. They may volunteer for challenging tasks, present ideas to managers, or take charge of team projects. Their willingness to stand out can be an asset when a company needs someone to propose fresh approaches. A Leo might say, "I can lead this campaign," and dive in with enthusiasm.

However, not all workplaces respond to boldness in the same way. Some might value calm, methodical teamwork more than a single person's drive. A Leo who does not adapt to that culture might clash with coworkers who feel overshadowed. They may need to learn how to share leadership, ask questions, and respect quieter voices. Balance is key: a Leo can use their confidence to motivate the team but must be careful not to drown out others' input.

When used well, a Leo's sense of self-assurance can help them climb career ladders. They might negotiate for better positions or propose big ideas to bosses. Yet, if they do not back up their boldness with solid work and strong relationships, they could appear as someone who talks big but does not deliver. To keep growing in a career, they need to pair confidence with consistent effort, teamwork, and openness to learning.

Romantic and Family Life

In personal relationships, Leos might be the ones to start a conversation with, "We should talk about our plans," or to plan a special evening. Their confidence can manifest as directness. They usually are not afraid to state how they feel, whether it is love, excitement, or concern about an issue. This can bring clarity to a relationship, as no one has to guess what the Leo is thinking.

Still, conflicts can arise if the Leo pushes too hard, assuming their preferences always take priority. A partner or family member might say, "I feel like you never consider my viewpoint." A balanced Leo learns to ask questions like, "How do you feel about this?" or "What would you like to do?" to ensure they are not dominating.

When confidence works in harmony with empathy, a Leo can become a supportive figure in the family, ready to handle emergencies or daily decisions. Their natural optimism can lift a house's atmosphere. A proud Leo parent might encourage children to explore their own talents, saying, "Go for it—you can do anything you set your mind to." Meanwhile, a romantic Leo might surprise a partner with thoughtful actions, trusting they can create memorable moments. Both examples show how healthy confidence can enrich personal ties.

Challenges to Leo Confidence

No one's confidence is unshakable, not even a Leo's. Certain events can unsettle their self-esteem. These might include:

Failure in a High-Profile Task: If a Leo takes on a big project—like organizing a major event—and it falls flat, they might feel deeply hurt, thinking they have let everyone down.

Harsh Criticism: Because they value respect, harsh or public criticism can cause a Leo to doubt themselves more than they might admit.

Comparison with Others: If they see a peer achieving more recognition or success, some Leos may feel overshadowed, even if they have their own accomplishments.

Loss of a Supportive Relationship: A breakup or a close friend moving away can strain their sense of stability. They might question their attractiveness or their ability to keep strong bonds.

When a Leo's confidence is knocked, they might react by withdrawing for a while or, conversely, by acting overly proud to hide their hurt. Some Leos might become short-tempered or defensive when they feel insecure. Recognizing these signs can help friends or family offer support at the right time.

Rebuilding Self-Esteem

If a Leo is feeling low, there are ways they can rebuild that sense of assurance:

Reflection on Past Wins: They can recall moments when they did well, whether small victories or big achievements. Remembering those times can remind them of their abilities.

Seeking Constructive Advice: Talking with a close friend, mentor, or counselor can offer perspective. Sometimes a new viewpoint helps a Leo see that one failure does not define them.

Focusing on Gradual Improvements: Setting small tasks or goals can boost a Leo's mood as they see progress. Rather than trying to fix everything at once, they can tackle bit-by-bit tasks.

Positive Self-Talk: As simple as it sounds, reminding themselves "I can handle challenges" or "I am capable of learning" can slowly rewire negative thoughts that arise after a setback.

These steps are not unique to Leos—anyone can benefit from them. But for a Leo, whose identity often ties in with pride or self-image, doing these things consistently can help them bounce back. Over time, they regain balance, remembering that they are more than one setback or one person's opinion.

Helping a Leo with Confidence

If someone close to you is a Leo who feels unsure, you can offer practical encouragement. Try:

Praising specific efforts: "I saw how you handled that meeting—you stayed calm under pressure," or "I love how you sketched that idea so clearly."

Offering kind reminders: "Even if it didn't work out this time, you learned something valuable. I know you'll use this lesson well."

Listening without judgment: Let them share fears or insecurities without dismissing or rushing to solve everything. Just hearing them out can ease some tension.

Involving them in group tasks: If they step away out of fear of failing again, gently invite them to smaller roles at first. Show them their input still matters.

Keep an eye on any sign they might prefer personal space. Some Leos might need time alone to think and recover. Overhelping can sometimes add pressure if they are not ready to talk. A balanced approach respects their independence but lets them know you have their back.

Healthy vs. Fragile Confidence

Not every display of pride signals true confidence. Sometimes, a Leo may have a more fragile sense of self, masked by loud behavior or constant bragging. This might happen if they never resolved underlying insecurities. A person with fragile confidence can seem unstoppable on the outside but is easily shaken by a minor criticism or a slight dip in attention.

In contrast, healthy confidence looks more stable. A Leo who has it can handle critique with a willingness to learn. They are open to the idea that not everyone will applaud them constantly. While they still love appreciation, their self-worth does not collapse if it does not happen. They can also celebrate other people's successes without feeling threatened, which is a sign their sense of self is not rooted in being the only star of the show.

Learning to Share the Spotlight

A typical growth point for Leos is realizing that sharing the spotlight does not reduce their own worth. This might mean letting others lead sometimes, praising teammates publicly, or giving credit where it is due. At first, a Leo might worry that if they are not at center stage, people will forget them. Over time, they can see that supporting others can earn just as much respect as commanding the stage alone.

Sharing the spotlight also means stepping aside when someone else is more knowledgeable or skilled in a particular area. For instance, if a friend is an expert at planning finances, a self-aware Leo can say, "You handle that part—you know it best." This does not lower their own standing; it shows a mature kind of leadership that recognizes different strengths in a group.

As Leos learn to give others room, they often discover that people appreciate their confidence more. Instead of viewing them as someone who hogs attention, friends and coworkers see them as a positive force that elevates everyone's talents. This shift can deepen the Leo's self-confidence because it is rooted in mutual respect, not in overshadowing others.

Balancing Confidence and Vulnerability

Because Leos tend to be strong-willed, they may feel uneasy revealing weaknesses or uncertainties. They might think, "I'm supposed to be the brave one—what if people see me struggling?" But true strength includes vulnerability. When a Leo feels safe to say, "I'm nervous about this" or "I don't have all the answers," it can bring relief. Others around them might step forward to help or to share advice.

Balancing confidence with vulnerability also builds deeper relationships. When a Leo only shows a tough front, it can create distance. Friends or family might think they cannot approach them with worries or that the Leo will judge them for being weak. But if the Leo occasionally admits, "I'm feeling uncertain," it signals to others that it is okay not to be perfect all the time.

This shift can help a Leo become more approachable. People might find it easier to share ideas or ask questions, knowing the Leo will not always dismiss them with, "I already know everything." Over time, the Leo's confidence can grow more secure, fueled by honest connections rather than a forced image of being fearless.

The Role of Self-Care

Confidence also depends on how well a Leo takes care of physical and emotional needs. If they are tired, stressed, or dealing with an unhealthy routine, they might snap at small problems or doubt themselves more easily. Simple habits, like getting enough rest, eating balanced meals, or exercising, can help keep them in a steady frame of mind.

Some Leos benefit from regular downtime—like reading, listening to music, or pursuing a quiet hobby. Although they often thrive in social settings, a little alone time can recharge them. Taking short breaks during a busy day keeps them from burning out, which in turn helps them stay at their best when they do take the lead.

Mental well-being also matters. If a Leo feels overwhelmed, they might talk to a trusted friend, counselor, or family member. Sharing the load can prevent bottled-up stress from chipping away at their confidence. Practicing mindfulness or basic relaxation techniques can also help them handle negative thoughts before they grow too large.

Public Image and Self-Belief

Leos often care about how they present themselves to the world. This might include style choices, social media presence, or professional reputation. While it is natural for them to want to look good, focusing too much on external image can sometimes make them vulnerable to outside opinions. If they rely on constant likes or compliments, their sense of worth can fluctuate.

Striking a balance is important. A healthy Leo can enjoy dressing well or sharing achievements online while knowing that these do not define their entire identity. If they receive negative comments, they can remind themselves that real self-belief comes from within. They can say, "I know my own capabilities," instead of letting one bad remark undo their self-assurance.

Leos who keep an inner compass—an understanding of their values and deeper goals—can navigate public reactions more calmly. They might appreciate praise, but they do not lose themselves if it is absent. They can accept criticism without crumbling because they know who they are, beyond a single performance or post.

Helping Others Feel Confident Too

A confident Leo in a group often becomes the one who boosts everyone else's morale. If they see a teammate doubting themselves, they might say, "I believe in you—look at what you've done before." This ability to lift others stems from their own sense of self; they are not afraid that someone else's success will dim their own light.

In friendships, a Leo can encourage a hesitant friend to try new hobbies, speak up in meetings, or stand up for their own rights. They might share stories of how they overcame fear. By showing genuine interest in a friend's progress, the Leo also expands their own confidence. Their leadership transforms from a solo act into a supportive environment.

Family members often benefit from this trait, too. A Leo might mentor younger siblings or offer practical advice to older relatives. Seeing the results—like a sibling who gains the courage to join a sports team—further strengthens the Leo's positive self-image. This cycle of lifting others while reinforcing their own confidence can create a warm and cooperative circle.

Watchouts: Overconfidence and Risks

Confidence is good, but overconfidence can lead to risky situations. A Leo who believes they can handle everything might take on projects beyond their resources or skills. They might think, "I'll do it all myself," only to realize too late that they need a team or more time. This can cause stress, burnout, or incomplete work.

Another danger is ignoring advice from others. Overly confident Leos might dismiss warnings, saying, "I know best," then run into avoidable problems. Balancing their self-belief with a willingness to learn ensures they do not sabotage themselves. Listening to trusted mentors, doing research, or testing a plan can help confirm if their idea is truly workable.

In personal life, overconfidence might appear as refusing to admit mistakes in relationships or finances. For instance, a Leo might overspend on something they believe will impress people, ignoring caution from a friend who says, "That might be too expensive." Admitting that caution was right can hurt their pride, but it can also prevent worse consequences. A little humility can protect them from bigger pitfalls.

Continual Growth of Leo Confidence

Confidence is not a fixed trait. It can evolve over a Leo's lifetime. As they face new challenges—changing careers, moving to a different place, or starting a family—they might discover fresh areas of doubt. But they also find opportunities to strengthen their belief in themselves by learning new skills or proving their resilience under stress.

A mature Leo often learns that true confidence does not mean never feeling afraid. Instead, it means acting even when fear is present, trusting that they can handle whatever comes next. They rely on past experiences to say, "I overcame that before, so I can manage this too." They also stay open to advice and adapt as needed, rather than insisting they are always right.

This maturity can spread to all parts of life. At work, they become a reliable force. In relationships, they show stability and care. In personal pursuits, they remain eager to push boundaries without overlooking the need for planning and learning. In short, their confidence becomes a balanced tool, not a showy performance.

Tips for Maintaining Balanced Self-Assurance

For Leos who want to keep a healthy sense of self-worth over time, here are some tips:

Reflect Often: Spend a few moments each week noting what went well and where there is room to grow. Recognize successes and allow space for mistakes.

Stay Curious: Learn from people around you. Even if you feel confident, hearing others' methods can refine your approach. Ask questions instead of pretending you know it all.

Accept Feedback: Not all feedback is pleasant, but some can be valuable. Sorting through criticism to find useful points helps you improve.

Support Others: By encouraging friends or coworkers, you reinforce your own abilities. Leading with kindness can bring out the best in everyone, including yourself.

Practice Self-Kindness: If you slip up, do not dwell too long in self-blame. Apologize if needed, make changes, and move on with renewed focus. Holding onto guilt can sap your confidence.

Over time, these habits can ground a Leo's confidence in real experience and empathy, rather than quick praise or short-lived triumphs.

CHAPTER 16: LEO AND EMOTIONS

Leos are often seen as vibrant and warm, radiating feelings that can brighten a room. Yet, emotions are complex, and a Leo's inner world can be both uplifting and challenging. This chapter looks at how Leos typically handle their emotions, from big bursts of enthusiasm to moments of hurt or sadness. We will also discuss the ways they connect with others emotionally, how they manage intense moods, and what can help them form healthy, deep bonds. By understanding these emotional layers, you can appreciate a Leo's heart in all its facets—both the sunshine it brings and the shadows it might hide.

The Heart at the Center

Astrologically, Leo is linked to the heart, symbolizing warmth, affection, and loyalty. These qualities often appear in a Leo's emotional life. Many Leos find it natural to show love or devotion to friends, partners, and causes they believe in. They might express this love through protective actions, caring words, or generous gestures. When a Leo says, "I care about you," they usually mean it with intensity.

This heart-centered approach also applies to how Leos handle group events or creative work. Their emotions often guide them. They might pick a project because it "feels right" rather than because it is the most logical option. This can lead to strong motivations or, sometimes, quick changes if that initial feeling fades.

At the same time, wearing their heart openly means Leos can be deeply affected by perceived slights or rejections. If they feel unloved or unappreciated, it can sting more than it would for some other signs. They might brood over a snub or a cold reply, wondering what they did wrong to lose that warmth.

Expressing Joy and Enthusiasm

One of the most noticeable emotional traits of many Leos is their ability to share joy in a lively way. If they are excited about a new project, everyone around them might know about it quickly. They might text friends, announce it on social media, or talk about it eagerly during lunch. Their happiness can be contagious, sparking interest among their circle.

Likewise, a Leo celebrating good news might go all out with gatherings, or at least share their excitement in a big way. The reason is simple: they love inviting others into their bright emotional state. It gives them energy to see people join in. While some might label this as seeking attention, often it is a genuine wish to spread positivity.

This enthusiastic nature helps them stay hopeful in difficult moments. Even if they face setbacks, many Leos bounce back by saying, "Next time, it will be even better." They cling to the possibility of success, trusting their own ability to rise again. This optimism can be a huge advantage when they are leading teams or supporting friends through rough patches.

Anger and Frustration

While Leos radiate warmth, they can also experience anger fiercely. Because they are protective of their pride and the people they love, threats or disrespect can set off strong reactions. A Leo might raise their voice, deliver sharp words, or walk away if they feel their dignity has been attacked. Some might slam doors or throw out a strong statement like, "I'm done with this!"

That said, anger often flares quickly and can subside just as fast once they feel heard or see an effort to make things right. If someone apologizes in a sincere way, a Leo may cool down, especially if they sense the apology respects their feelings. They might say something like, "I appreciate your honesty. Let's move forward."

However, if the conflict involves betrayal—like a broken promise or a disloyal act—Leos can take much longer to forgive. Betrayal cuts deeply into their sense of trust. They may hold onto anger or bitterness for a while, sometimes waiting for a clear sign of regret before softening.

Handling Sadness and Disappointment

Sadness can appear for a Leo when their high expectations or desires do not match reality. For instance, if a creative effort fails or a friend withdraws, they might feel sadness that runs beneath their usual sunny demeanor. Some Leos hide this behind humor or busy schedules, not wanting to show vulnerability.

Yet, ignoring sadness can lead to deeper emotional strain. A wise Leo learns that expressing sadness can bring relief. That might mean confiding in someone they trust, writing down their feelings, or quietly reflecting on what went wrong. By acknowledging sadness, they prevent it from growing into cynicism or resentment.

Family and close friends can help by offering understanding and empathy, instead of quickly saying, "Cheer up" or "You'll get over it." A Leo might need a supportive ear to talk through their disappointment. Once they feel genuinely heard, their natural optimism can start to re-emerge, allowing them to plan their next steps.

Fear and Insecurity

Even though Leos are known for boldness, they are not immune to fear. Sometimes they fear failing in front of others or worry about losing respect. They might also fear that if they open up too much, people will reject them. These worries can be hidden behind a confident exterior, because they do not want others to see them as weak.

When fear builds up, Leos might avoid taking certain risks or become defensive. For instance, a Leo who fears failure might say, "I don't care about that project anyway," when in truth, they care a lot. Recognizing these patterns is key. A Leo might learn to say to themselves, "I'm feeling nervous because I want this to work out," rather than denying it.

They can also benefit from positive self-reminders: "I've succeeded in many things before," or "It's okay to fail sometimes—at least I tried." Talking to a trusted friend or mentor can also ease their insecurities. Hearing someone else say, "You have what it takes," can give them the push they need to face their fears more openly.

Emotional Sensitivity to Criticism

Leos value respect, so any criticism—especially if harsh—can sting. When they receive feedback that seems cold or insulting, they might react with anger or sadness. This sensitivity does not mean they cannot learn from critique, but the delivery matters. If they feel attacked, their first response might be to defend themselves rather than listen.

To handle this sensitivity, Leos can practice separating the critique from their sense of worth. They can ask, "Is this feedback about my work or my character?" Often, a criticism is about a specific action, not about who they are as a person. By focusing on the practical side—like improving a certain skill—they can keep their self-esteem intact.

Friends or colleagues giving feedback can help by framing it in a balanced way: "I appreciate your hard work on this, and here's one area we could make even better." That approach validates what they have done well while pointing out improvements. Leos often respond more cooperatively to such fairness.

Passion in Relationships

When it comes to romantic or close friendships, Leos can be quite passionate. They like big gestures, affectionate words, and clear expressions of love. If they truly care for someone, they may plan surprises, show open admiration, and defend that person against any perceived harm. Their emotional intensity can feel thrilling—like a bright fire.

However, this passion also means a Leo can become jealous or possessive if they suspect a threat to the relationship. They might say, "Are you sure you still want me around?" or "Why are you spending so much time with that person?" if they feel insecure. Healthy communication is vital here. A partner or friend who calmly reassures them, "You are important, and I'm not replacing you," can ease those worries.

Leos thrive on mutual respect in relationships. They do not mind sharing love and warmth, but they also need to feel valued. If they sense a one-sided dynamic, where they give attention but get little in return, they might become resentful. Balancing their strong emotional contributions with a partner or friend's reciprocation leads to a steady bond.

Emotional Support for Others

A well-grounded Leo is often ready to help loved ones handle emotional burdens. If a friend is upset, a Leo might sit down, offer comforting words, or think of practical solutions. Their warmth can be a healing presence, as they genuinely care about the people they consider part of their "pride."

They may also attempt to protect friends from negative situations, saying, "You deserve better than that," or stepping in if they see someone being treated poorly. This protective instinct can be positive, though occasionally it might become overwhelming if the friend wants to handle things on their own. Learning to gauge when a friend needs help and when they need space is part of a Leo's emotional growth.

By offering support, Leos can form very tight-knit relationships. They often become the "go-to" person when someone needs encouragement. This role can boost the Leo's own sense of purpose, reinforcing a cycle in which they feel proud to care and others feel grateful for the care given.

Dealing with Emotional Overload

Leos can sometimes feel too much at once: joy, frustration, worry, excitement. When life events pile up—such as a work deadline, a family conflict, and a personal setback—these strong emotions can collide. A Leo might become moody or lash out if they do not find ways to manage the overload.

Healthy coping strategies can help. Some Leos benefit from physical outlets—like a brisk walk, dancing, or a brief workout—to release pent-up energy. Others prefer creative outlets, such as painting, writing, or playing music to channel strong feelings. Talking to a close friend or counselor can also reduce emotional strain.

A key step is recognizing early signs of overload: trouble sleeping, irritability, or feeling restless. If a Leo can pause and say, "I'm getting overwhelmed—I need a moment," they are less likely to explode later. Scheduling downtime or quieter activities might feel unnatural at first, but it can prevent bigger emotional meltdowns.

Emotional Honesty and Openness

Many Leos value honesty in how they express emotions. They typically do not enjoy being vague or playing mind games. Instead, they might say, "I'm upset with you because of what happened," or "I really like you," or "I feel ignored." This directness can be refreshing, because people rarely have to guess what the Leo thinks or feels.

However, a Leo's bluntness can catch others off-guard if it appears too sudden or intense. For instance, a coworker might be taken aback if a Leo says, "I'm really frustrated with how you handled that report," without softening the tone. Balancing direct honesty with a considerate approach can help a Leo share emotions without causing misunderstandings.

In personal relationships, emotional openness often creates deeper trust. A partner who knows exactly where the Leo stands can respond more effectively. That said, it is still important for a Leo to ask about the other person's feelings in return. True emotional openness is a two-way street, not just a Leo stating their side.

Healing Emotional Wounds

When a Leo experiences heartbreak—such as a betrayal, a lost relationship, or any major disappointment—it can leave them feeling like their light has dimmed. The emotional pain might linger, especially if they see it as an attack on their pride. Healing can be gradual, requiring self-reflection and a willingness to let go of anger or hurt.

Some steps for healing might include:

Admitting the Hurt: Recognizing that the pain is real. Instead of brushing it aside, say, "I feel wounded because of this situation."

Allowing Sadness or Anger: For a short period, letting those emotions exist can help them pass rather than burying them.

Finding Meaning or Lessons: A Leo might ask, "What can I learn from this?" or "What do I need in future friendships or partnerships?"

Reconnecting with Passions: Doing creative work, socializing with supportive friends, or revisiting hobbies can restore a sense of joy.

Over time, a Leo who processes a deep hurt often comes out stronger, with a refined idea of what they truly want and who they want to be around. Though scars may remain, these can act as reminders of lessons learned.

Emotional Boundaries

While Leos give a lot of emotional energy, they also need personal boundaries to stay balanced. If friends or relatives rely too heavily on the Leo's warmth, it can drain them. A Leo might feel like they are always the one to cheer people up, with nobody returning that care. Eventually, resentment or emotional fatigue can set in.

Setting boundaries might mean politely saying, "I can't talk right now—I need some time for myself," or "I'm sorry, but I can't handle your issue alone. Maybe we should find additional help." These statements might feel awkward at first, but they protect the Leo from constant emotional demands that exceed their capacity.

Likewise, if a Leo is giving too much advice or stepping into people's problems uninvited, they may need to learn to let others solve their own issues. This is part of respecting others' boundaries. Not everyone wants a bold helper all the time. Finding that balance keeps the Leo from feeling rejected if someone says, "Thanks, but I can handle it myself."

Understanding Mood Swings

All humans have mood shifts, but the contrast might be more noticeable for a Leo because of their generally bright disposition. If they wake up feeling low or something triggers frustration during the day, the drop from sunny to stormy can seem dramatic. Friends might ask, "What happened? You were so cheerful an hour ago!"

Being aware of these swings can help a Leo handle them better. Sometimes, it is just a normal reaction to stress, disappointment, or physical tiredness. Recognizing triggers—like lack of sleep, hunger, or an unresolved personal issue—can prevent the mood from spiraling. A quick snack, short rest, or a honest talk might reset their emotional balance.

Friends and partners should remember not to take these swings too personally. Offering calm support or space to breathe is often more effective than demanding they snap out of it. Usually, once a Leo processes whatever is bothering them, their mood can rise back to a warmer place.

Empathy and Sensitivity to Others' Feelings

While a Leo's own feelings can be quite strong, many of them also show empathy to those who struggle. They might sense when a friend is hiding sadness or see tension in a coworker's body language. Their own experience of big emotions helps them spot signs of unrest in others.

That said, empathy is not automatic. A Leo can become self-focused if they get too caught up in their own drama. If they forget to check in with loved ones, they could miss signals that someone else needs help. A mindful Leo balances their emotional world with the needs of those around them, asking, "How are you feeling?" or "Do you want to talk?"

By practicing active listening, they can strengthen bonds. When a friend shares their worries, a caring Leo might respond, "I hear you. That sounds difficult—tell me more," showing genuine interest. This not only helps the friend but also enriches the Leo's personal growth as they learn to offer compassion in real moments.

Emotional Growth Over Time

Like anyone, a Leo's emotional patterns can shift as they gather more life experience. Younger Leos might be quicker to show dramatic highs and lows, while older ones might channel their emotions into more thoughtful expressions. They might learn that not every feeling needs to be acted upon immediately, especially anger or impulsive excitement.

A mature Leo may also become more skilled at picking which emotional causes to invest in deeply. Instead of scattering energy on many small things, they might focus on a few goals or relationships that matter most. This selectivity can help them maintain emotional balance and avoid burning out from constant intensity.

They also learn from past emotional missteps—like times they hurt someone with harsh words or neglected a friend because they were too wrapped up in their own issues. Accepting responsibility for those moments and adjusting behavior shows real emotional maturity. Over time, they become a supportive figure who combines boldness with empathy, resilience, and humility.

Conflict Resolution and Forgiveness

When emotional tensions build into conflicts, a Leo might respond with strong words. Yet, if they value the connection, they usually prefer resolving the dispute eventually rather than letting it linger. They might seek a direct talk, saying, "Let's clear the air," or "We need to settle this."

Approaches to conflict resolution include:

Listening Time: Each person gets a set amount of time to speak without interruption.

Clarifying Intent: A Leo might ask, "What did you mean by that comment?" to avoid jumping to conclusions.

Owning Mistakes: If the Leo went too far, apologizing can open the door for the other side to soften.

Suggesting a Path Forward: "Let's agree to do this differently next time," or "Can we meet halfway?"

Forgiveness can be a process. If trust was broken, it might take repeated signs of good faith to mend the relationship. But a Leo who sees genuine regret often releases resentment to avoid holding onto negative feelings. Moving on can restore their emotional sunshine, which they prefer over long-term grudges.

The Role of Hobbies in Emotional Well-Being

Hobbies that let Leos express themselves can serve as emotional outlets. Singing, painting, dancing, writing—these creative forms let them pour out feelings without always having to talk about them. Even physically active hobbies like sports or yoga can help them release tension stored in the body.

When a Leo invests time in such pursuits, they often come back to daily life feeling calmer and more focused. They might also share these hobbies with friends, turning them into social connections. For example, a Leo who loves dance might invite others to a casual dance class, turning a personal passion into a communal activity.

If a Leo neglects these outlets, their emotions might build up with no place to go. That can result in irritability or dissatisfaction. Encouraging them to keep up with their personal interests can be a subtle way of helping them maintain emotional balance. They might say afterward, "I'm so glad I took that hour to paint. I feel better now."

Practicing Self-Compassion

Leos often hold themselves to high standards, expecting to be the best or at least highly effective in whatever they do. When they fall short of their own expectations, harsh self-criticism might appear. They might think, "I should never fail," or "I let everyone down." Self-compassion is the antidote here. It means treating themselves with the same kindness they would offer a friend who is struggling.

Self-compassion can involve noticing negative thoughts and responding with understanding. "I messed up, but I'm human—this is a chance to learn." It might also mean allowing themselves a break after a stressful period rather than pushing onward until exhaustion. By practicing self-compassion, Leos keep their emotional spirits healthy, reducing the risk of burnout.

Taking a step back to reflect on achievements, big or small, can also remind a Leo that they are more than this one setback. "I've done many things right in the past, so I can do well again." This internal reassurance strengthens their emotional resilience.

CHAPTER 17: LEO IN DIFFERENT STAGES OF LIFE

Leos often show a spirited way of being, no matter their age. Still, how that spirit unfolds can vary as they move from childhood to old age. A young Leo might reveal curiosity and eagerness, while a teen Leo could show more dramatic expressions of self. An adult Leo might shape a career around leadership, and an older Leo might share wisdom through storytelling and guidance. In this chapter, we will look at the typical traits of Leos at each life stage, noting the challenges and rewards that can appear as they grow. Even though everyone's path is unique, these patterns often help us see how Leos evolve over time.

Leo as a Young Child

Early Joy and Curiosity
Many Leo children shine bright from a young age. They may enjoy performing songs, reading lines from a story out loud, or dancing around the living room. If they have siblings, they might take the lead in games, thinking of creative plots and inviting others to join. They often look for approval from parents, grandparents, and teachers, lighting up when they are told, "Great job!"

Love of Play and Make-Believe
Because Leos have an active imagination, they often invent pretend stories or create mini-dramas with toys. They might make up entire scenes where they are the main character. In preschool or early school, this can help them learn new things in a fun way. They might volunteer to be the star in a simple class play or happily show their

art to the teacher. Adults can support them by providing open-ended materials—like costumes, craft supplies, or building sets—that give them room to be imaginative.

Early Tendency to Lead

In a group of children, a Leo might step forward, organizing how to play house or pirates. Other children could willingly follow, or they could push back. If a Leo child becomes bossy, small clashes can happen. Helping them learn the difference between leading kindly and being too forceful is important. Parents can suggest language like, "How about we all decide together?" or "Let's take turns being in charge," which balances the Leo child's natural drive with fairness.

Need for Guidance and Boundaries

While Leo children enjoy compliments, they also need rules to keep them from feeling lost. A parent or teacher who sets clear limits—like consistent bedtime or polite behavior rules—offers the child security. If a Leo child starts to think they can do whatever they want without consequence, it might encourage stubbornness. Balanced feedback—praise for good behavior plus calm consequences for breaking rules—can keep them confident but respectful of others.

Leo as a Teen

Emerging Identity and Style

During the teen years, many Leos experiment with personal style. They might pick bold clothing, try unique hairstyles, or join clubs that let them shine. They may enjoy activities like drama, sports, or music, where they can show off skills. Getting noticed by peers can feel very rewarding, though it can also invite envy or teasing. A teen Leo should learn how to stand strong without putting down classmates who have different strengths.

Emotional Intensity

Teen Leos might show big highs—excited about friendships, interests, or romantic feelings—and equally big lows if faced with rejection or conflict. They can be dramatic when upset, sometimes writing emotional posts on social media or locking themselves in a room. Parents can be supportive by gently hearing them out rather than brushing off their strong reactions. Encouraging a teen Leo to channel that energy into healthy outlets—like art, sports, or volunteering—can prevent emotional overwhelm.

Need for Respectful Independence

As Leos gain more awareness of themselves, they might demand freedom to make choices. This can include picking school courses, developing a personal schedule, or deciding on social plans. Although they wish to break free from total adult control, they still need boundaries. Parents can say, "I trust your decisions, but I'm here to guide you if you need it." Striking this balance helps teen Leos learn responsibility without feeling stifled.

Possible Peer Pressure

With a strong need for approval, a teen Leo might be tempted to do risky things to stay in the spotlight. They may want to impress peers or maintain a certain image. Adult figures can remind them that real confidence comes from within, not just from a dare or a sudden impulse. Suggesting safe ways to stand out—like joining a creative project or leading a community event—can channel their energy positively.

Leo in Early Adulthood

Carving Out a Life Path

Young adult Leos often approach the world with excitement. They might move out to attend college, start a job, or pick up apprenticeships. Their natural charm could help them find mentors or network easily. Some may enter fields that welcome their leadership—like business, event planning, the arts, or education. Others might choose creative paths, feeling driven to express original ideas.

Balancing Ambition and Realities

One challenge for young adult Leos is managing high ambition with real-world constraints. They might dream of instant success—owning a business, making a mark in a chosen field, or traveling widely. But real life often requires patience, skill-building, and saving money. A wise Leo learns to break large goals into smaller steps while staying open to feedback. Mentors can remind them that setbacks do not define them, only teach them new lessons.

Relationships and Friendships

Early adulthood is a time when Leos may meet many different people, forming close bonds with those who appreciate their warmth. They often enjoy hosting gatherings—like house parties or get-togethers at restaurants. However, they should look out for friends who might use them for freebies or constant entertainment. True friends will support a Leo's dreams but also stand beside them during setbacks.

First Serious Responsibilities

Many Leos start taking on major responsibilities at this age—rent, car payments, or even a small business. This can be a test of their ability to handle details. Though they have big ideas, they might find repetitive tasks dull. Learning to manage finances, meet deadlines, and keep track of schedules is crucial. Leos who succeed in these areas usually do so by blending creativity (like innovative budgeting methods) with discipline (like consistent reminders or apps that track tasks).

Leo in the Prime of Adulthood

Leading and Influencing
 By the time they reach the middle of their adult years, many Leos have honed their talents and found a niche. They might be leaders in a workplace, community group, or family setting. Their confidence, built from experiences, can make them trusted problem-solvers. Whether they run a department at work or lead a volunteer team, they often combine optimism with practical know-how.

Deepening Personal Bonds
 In relationships, a Leo at this stage often values loyalty and stability. If they have a partner or family, they might invest in making the home comfortable and lively, organizing everything from small weekend outings to holiday traditions. Their protective side grows stronger; they want loved ones to feel safe and proud. This can make them excellent cheerleaders for a spouse's or child's pursuits, as they pour energy into ensuring the family thrives.

Handling Setbacks with Maturity
 By now, many Leos have encountered enough ups and downs to know life is not always sunny. They might have faced job changes, health scares, or complicated family issues. A mature Leo recognizes that a setback can be overcome with patience. They will likely draw on their personal network or mentors for advice, and they are more willing to admit they do not have every answer. This balanced humility helps them navigate tough times without losing their core spark.

Maintaining Balance
 One thing adult Leos often work on is balancing personal ambition with family or community needs. They might have to decide between chasing a higher position at work or spending more time with their kids. They could also realize that being a good leader

means giving others space to shine. If they do this thoughtfully, they become respected figures who empower others rather than overshadow them.

Leo in Later Years

Sharing Wisdom and Experience

Older Leos often step into a guiding role for the younger generation. Whether it is younger relatives, community members, or coworkers, they enjoy passing along lessons learned from years of leading, creating, or problem-solving. They might become mentors who encourage risk-taking in a positive way, telling stories of how they faced their own challenges. Their warmth and sense of humor can make these stories uplifting rather than lecturing.

Adapting to New Pace

With time, a Leo's energy might slow a bit, but their will to live fully remains. They could find joy in simpler activities—spending hours reading, gardening, or hosting small gatherings at home. Some may embrace grandparenthood with enthusiasm, playing actively with grandchildren or cheering them on at events. The key is finding ways to keep that Leo spark going, even if they are no longer running around as much.

Reflecting on Achievements and Legacy

Older Leos often look back on their accomplishments. Some may feel proud of a long career, a happy family, or a creative project that spanned decades. Others might regret not taking certain chances. Overall, a Leo who has stayed true to themselves can feel satisfied, seeing how their warmth and leadership touched many lives. They might also write memoirs, paint memories, or do other reflective tasks, using their creativity to capture precious experiences.

Continued Desire for Appreciation

Even as they age, many Leos still enjoy hearing, "We value your help and guidance." A simple thank-you or a request for advice can lift their spirits, showing that they remain an important part of the community. In groups, older Leos might lead smaller activities or give inspirational talks. If they sense that no one wants their input, they might feel sidelined. Friends and family can help by inviting them to share stories or join discussions, making sure their lion heart continues to feel seen.

Challenges and Growth Across the Years

Needing to Adjust to Change
One thread through all these stages is dealing with life changes. Moving from one level of schooling to another, switching jobs, or going through family transitions can shake a Leo's sense of stability. Because they often like feeling in control, surprises might unsettle them. Over time, they learn that adapting can bring fresh opportunities, and that being flexible does not weaken their strong spirit.

Facing Self-Doubt
While many see Leos as brimming with confidence, times of self-doubt can pop up at any age. A school-age Leo might worry about not being liked by peers. A teenage Leo might question their identity. An adult Leo might fear they have not used their potential fully, and an older Leo might feel irrelevant as younger folks take center stage. Recognizing and normalizing these doubts can be healthier than pretending they do not exist.

Developing Emotional Maturity
From the strong-willed toddler to the wise elder, all Leos benefit from learning emotional balance. Early in life, they might have dramatic mood swings—angry outbursts or giddy highs. Later, they pick up ways to talk about feelings calmly, listen to others, and share the spotlight. This progression does not happen automatically; it

takes guidance from mentors, friends, or self-reflection. But as Leos grow emotionally, they become kinder leaders who can guide families, teams, or communities with care.

Holding Onto Creativity and Passion

A big joy for many Leos is their ability to keep creative flames alive. Whether that means painting, writing poems, or sharing family recipes, the chance to express themselves can run through all phases of life. Some might change mediums—maybe as a teen they wrote short stories, and in adulthood, they design gardens. The main theme is that creativity feeds their soul. Encouraging them to keep this spark is key, no matter the age.

Advice for Each Stage

For Leo Children: Parents and teachers can offer room for self-expression. Let them show off artwork or lead small parts of a class project. Also, teach them gently to respect peers' ideas.

For Teen Leos: Support them in exploring interests—like drama club, music, art, or sports—while reminding them of their limits. Encourage them to try new things without fear of looking silly. Keep communication open so they feel safe sharing doubts.

For Young Adults: Suggest they seek mentors at work or college to channel their ambition wisely. Urge them to balance big ideas with practical steps and good planning. Emphasize self-awareness: confidence is great, but listening is just as vital.

For Midlife Leos: Help them refine their leadership style. If they are parents, show how to let their children develop individuality. In careers, highlight the value of collaboration. Also, encourage them to find hobbies that relieve stress, so they do not burn out.

For Older Leos: Remind them that wisdom and guiding others can be deeply fulfilling. Show them new ways to connect—like online groups or local committees—if physical activities slow down. Embrace their stories and let them share. Thank them for their contributions so they still feel valued.

Key Transitions

Finishing School or Formal Training

Graduation often marks a big leap for a Leo, moving from a structured environment to a more flexible one. They might need to face competition or decide on a career track. Harnessing their flair for leadership can help them stand out in interviews or job hunts. Yet, they must also show real teamwork skills to avoid looking like they only care about personal glory.

Forming Lasting Relationships

Whether it is a long-term friendship group or a romantic partnership, forming steady emotional bonds is a milestone. A Leo might initially be drawn to people who admire them, but true closeness develops when they learn to respect others' needs equally. This could mean practicing compromise or supporting a partner's dreams, not just focusing on their own.

Parenthood or Mentoring Roles

A Leo who becomes a parent can transfer that joyful energy into raising a child. They might plan fun parties, read bedtime stories with dramatic voices, and cheer on every milestone. Mentoring at work or in a community club can similarly satisfy their protective and caring side. Yet, these roles also require them to handle frustration calmly—children and mentees will not always follow their lead perfectly.

Retirement or Reduced Work

Later in life, stepping back from full-time duties might unsettle a

Leo who is used to being in charge. They might fear losing the sense of purpose that came from work. Finding new avenues—like volunteering, creative projects, or spending time with grandchildren—keeps that light shining. They can channel leadership into smaller events or local associations that value their experience.

Consistent Traits Over Time

Throughout all these changes, certain Leo characteristics often remain:

Warmth and Charisma: They like to make others smile, whether they are six years old or sixty.

Pride and Confidence: Most Leos hold onto a strong sense of self-worth, even when life challenges them.

Love of Creativity: They usually keep some form of artistic or imaginative activity in their world.

Desire for Appreciation: Feeling recognized matters, though they might handle it differently at various ages.

Protective Nature: They stand up for loved ones or for causes they believe in, showing loyalty in all chapters of life.

Potential Pitfalls to Watch For

Stubbornness: A Leo might refuse to adapt, ignoring wise advice. This can stall growth if they cling to old methods that no longer work.

Excessive Pride: At any age, a Leo can become closed to suggestions, thinking they already know best. This can harm relationships or career progress.

Fear of Appearing Weak: They might hide struggles, missing the chance for support. Over time, bottled-up worries can lead to burnout or conflict.

Overcommitment: Trying to please everyone or maintain a top role in multiple spheres (work, home, community) can exhaust them. They need to learn to say no sometimes.

Difficulty Accepting Loss of Authority: Especially in later stages, stepping aside to let younger people lead can be hard. If they do not let go gracefully, friction can arise.

Embracing Each Stage

Ultimately, a Leo's life is not just about shining in one period but finding healthy ways to adapt and grow through each shift. In childhood, that might mean learning to share the spotlight. In the teen years, it might mean finding ways to express big emotions safely. As adults, it involves balancing personal goals with community or family needs. In older age, it might be about offering guidance without trying to control everything.

What remains is the essential Leo spirit: a bright, lion-like heart that loves creativity, connection, and a chance to show kindness or leadership. If each stage is treated as an opportunity to refine these qualities—rather than a time to cling to past glories—a Leo can remain a source of warmth for themselves and for those around them. Their story becomes one of real growth, weaving together confidence and empathy as they pass through each phase of life.

CHAPTER 18: LEO'S HOBBIES AND SKILLS

Leos often carry a bold spirit into all that they do, and this can shape the hobbies and skills they choose. Whether it is in music, art, sports, or community work, they usually gravitate toward activities that let them express their creativity or leadership. In this chapter, we will look at common interests Leos might enjoy, why these pursuits appeal to their nature, and how they can build their abilities in a balanced way. We will also note potential pitfalls—like overstretching themselves or seeking too much attention. By understanding the link between Leos and certain hobbies, you can see how they channel their bright energy into fun, mastery, and personal growth.

Love for the Performing Arts

Music and Theater
Leos often find themselves drawn to performance. They may enjoy singing, acting, playing an instrument, or dancing onstage. The chance to shine in front of an audience can be exhilarating, tapping into their natural flair. A Leo singer might relish taking solos in a choir, while a drama-loving Leo could thrive in school plays or local theater. Applause feels validating, but so does the creative flow itself.

Developing Stage Presence
Performing arts require more than raw passion. Mastery comes from regular practice, vocal or acting lessons, and learning to handle stage nerves. A Leo who invests this effort can gain both skill and confidence. They might enter local talent shows, audition for a

community play, or join a band. Over time, they learn to refine technique rather than just relying on charm.

Avoiding Spotlight Overload
One risk here is letting the applause become the main motivation. If a Leo bases self-worth solely on standing ovations, they might struggle when applause is absent. Healthy performers learn to enjoy the process of rehearsing and improving. They also share the stage with fellow artists, recognizing that teamwork often produces the best shows. A humble approach keeps them from appearing arrogant.

Artistic Creations

Painting, Drawing, and Crafts
Many Leos feel inspired to put images or ideas onto paper or canvas. Their preference might be bright colors, bold lines, or dramatic scenes that echo their lively nature. Some may lean toward painting large murals, while others prefer detailed sketches. Crafts like jewelry-making or pottery can also let them produce unique items that reflect personal style.

Why It Appeals
Artistic hobbies let Leos share their inner world without speaking. They might capture emotions in a painting—using wide strokes and vivid hues that symbolize how they feel. The chance to stand out through style is big here. A Leo might gift homemade art to friends or display pieces in local shows, feeling proud that their personal vision is on view.

Balancing Practice and Show
Art demands patience, trial-and-error, and studying techniques. A Leo who jumps straight to final pieces without refining basics might become frustrated if results do not match their bold ideas. But if they respect the learning process, they can grow quickly. Positive

feedback from teachers or mentors fuels them, but they should also be ready for constructive critiques that lead to better skills.

Sports and Physical Activities

Team Sports
Leos can be drawn to sports where they can both shine individually and contribute to a group. Basketball, soccer, or volleyball might give them a platform to show quick moves and leadership. They could become team captains, coordinating plays, or giving motivational pep talks before games. The excitement of a roaring crowd or supportive teammates lights up a Leo's competitive spirit.

Individual Challenges
On the other hand, some Leos prefer individual sports like tennis, boxing, or track, where their personal achievements take center stage. Winning a match or setting a record can feel like a proud moment they have earned by their own effort. However, they must remain open to sportsmanship—showing respect to opponents and learning from losses.

Staying Active for Health
Not every Leo aims to be a sports star. Some engage in activities like hiking, dancing, or martial arts purely for fun and fitness. Moving the body helps them channel energy and maintain emotional balance. They might join dance fitness classes or take up a martial art that teaches discipline. The key is staying consistent, which means finding an activity they truly enjoy rather than forcing themselves into something just for show.

Public Speaking and Debate

Being the Voice
Leos often have a knack for speaking up, which can translate into a hobby like public speaking or debate. They might join a debate club,

a speech team, or local events that let them discuss topics in front of an audience. Expressing thoughts clearly and persuasively can be thrilling, feeding that natural desire to be heard.

Building Skills

Success in public speaking demands more than confidence. A Leo also needs strong research, clear organization, and the ability to listen to opposing viewpoints. By practicing these, they grow as communicators. They learn how to structure arguments, use facts effectively, and address counterpoints calmly rather than just relying on a powerful voice.

Leading Workshops

As they refine their speaking ability, some Leos may move into teaching or workshop leading. They could give presentations at local clubs, schools, or community centers on topics they care about. This role satisfies their leadership drive while contributing to the community. Still, a humble touch—inviting questions, acknowledging other opinions—helps keep the tone welcoming rather than bossy.

Organizing Events and Gatherings

Party Planning and Coordination

With a flair for creating memorable experiences, Leos might enjoy planning events—birthday gatherings, family reunions, local fundraisers. They put effort into decorations, themes, and activities, aiming to see everyone smiling. Friends might rely on the Leo to arrange a game night or a special dinner because they know it will be lively and creative.

Volunteer or Charity Events

Leos can extend these talents to community causes, like organizing donation drives or local fests. In these roles, they not only showcase leadership but also channel it into good deeds. Seeing a large turnout can spark pride, especially if the event helps others. This sense of purpose goes beyond personal accolades, letting them give back in a way that matches their outgoing nature.

Balancing the Details

Planning big gatherings can be stressful. A Leo might have grand ideas but forget the budget or scheduling constraints. Creating a detailed checklist can prevent last-minute chaos. Delegating tasks is also wise—harnessing the help of others prevents a Leo from feeling alone in the workload. Letting team members shine in their own areas can lead to smoother, more harmonious events.

Teaching and Mentoring

Guiding Others

As Leos mature, some discover that one of their favorite ways to spend time is sharing what they know. They might tutor younger students in math, lead workshops on art techniques, or teach a sport to beginners. They get satisfaction from watching someone's face light up with new understanding, feeling proud that they played a part.

Encouraging Confidence

A skilled Leo mentor knows how to encourage shy or unsure learners. They might say, "I was once in your shoes, and look where I am now," offering a living example of growth. Their own experience with confidence helps them guide others to push past doubts. They can share tips on how to present oneself or how to stand firm in new endeavors.

Avoiding Over-Domination

Sometimes, a Leo might overshadow the learner by talking too much or showing off. Striking a balance means letting the student try, make mistakes, and discover strengths on their own path. A humble teacher steps back once they have given instructions or advice, allowing the person to progress. After all, the goal is to empower, not to prove the teacher's greatness.

Community Leadership

Local Clubs and Organizations
Leos may find a home in organizations that encourage them to plan and lead. They might join a civic club, become part of the school board, or volunteer for a local arts council. In these spaces, they can propose new ideas—like a neighborhood clean-up day or a youth art contest. They typically enjoy bringing people together for a shared purpose.

Political or Social Advocacy
Some Leos step beyond day-to-day activities and venture into social or political causes. They might speak at town meetings, rally for local improvements, or coordinate donation efforts for community issues. Leading such initiatives can be demanding but also rewarding when they see real impact. Their fiery nature helps them persevere, although they should stay open to compromise to achieve broader support.

Keeping Ego in Check
In leadership roles, a Leo might struggle if they let personal praise overshadow the group's mission. They should remember that true leadership focuses on results and the well-being of the community, not just on applause. Encouraging other voices, celebrating group wins, and sharing credit all help them stay balanced and effective.

Writing and Storytelling

Creative Writing
Leos who prefer quieter self-expression might turn to writing stories, poems, or scripts. This can be an outlet for their vivid imagination. They may create characters who share their bold traits

or who face dramatic plots that reflect a Leo's emotional intensity. Whether they share these works online, publish them, or keep them personal, the creative process can bring joy.

Memoirs and Biographies

Some Leos enjoy writing about real events—sharing personal experiences in blogs or short essays. If they have led an interesting life journey, they might record it for younger generations. True stories of challenges and successes can offer inspiration to others. Plus, writing them out helps a Leo reflect on lessons learned.

Storytelling Performances

If a Leo pairs writing with performance, they could do spoken word shows, story slams, or open-mic nights. This blends the love of narration with the thrill of an audience. The audience's reactions—gasps, laughter, applause—fuel the Leo's desire to share more. It is vital, though, that they welcome feedback and keep refining their craft rather than just enjoying the spotlight.

Traveling and Cultural Exploration

Ventures for Inspiration

Some Leos love exploring new places as a way to feed creativity and meet different people. They might visit various regions, try local foods, and observe cultural events to spark fresh ideas for art, writing, or community projects. A bold Leo might plan group trips, acting as the fun coordinator who organizes schedules and activities.

Sharing Discoveries

Upon returning, a Leo might create photo slideshows, blog posts, or casual presentations to share what they saw. This is not just to gain attention; it can also spread knowledge about other cultures or ways of living. They might introduce new cooking recipes, show local crafts, or highlight music styles that fascinated them. Their enthusiasm can open friends' eyes to the richness of the wider world.

Money and Practical Considerations

Not all Leos can hop on a plane whenever they want. They need to plan trips, set budgets, and possibly travel in a group. If finances are tight, they might find local getaways or day trips that still bring novelty. Learning to enjoy simpler adventures can keep them from feeling bored. The main point is experiencing something different, not necessarily going far away.

Technology and Digital Spaces

Online Content Creation

Some Leos find a stage in the digital world. They might run a YouTube channel, podcast, or social media page, where they share tips, talk about life, or present comedic skits. Their naturally outgoing style can draw viewers or listeners. Positive feedback fuels them, while negative comments test their resilience.

Gaming and E-Sports

Leos with a competitive streak might like online gaming, particularly games that emphasize teamwork or strategy. They could form teams, lead discussions on tactics, and relish the excitement of matches. Streaming gameplay can also become a form of performance. But it is important to watch out for toxic interactions or spending too many hours in front of a screen.

Balancing Virtual and Real Life

While online spaces can offer recognition, a Leo should also keep real-world ties strong. Friends and family might miss them if they spend all free time on the computer. A balanced schedule—some online fun mixed with offline gatherings—keeps their social world broad. This approach also helps them maintain healthy boundaries, so they do not wrap all self-esteem in digital likes or follows.

Collecting and Showcasing

Collecting Hobbies
Leos who love visual appeal might develop a collecting hobby. It could be rare coins, action figures, vintage clothing, or art pieces. They enjoy picking items that stand out, then arranging them in eye-catching ways. If they can show these collections at gatherings or in an online gallery, it might feel fulfilling.

Creative Display
They might get creative about how they display items—using glass cases with lights, color-coding, or crafting unique shelves. Inviting guests to see the collection becomes a mini event. The Leo might tell stories about each piece, why it matters, or where they found it, weaving their natural showmanship into the hobby.

Remembering Practical Limits
Collecting can be fun, but it can also get expensive or take up lots of space. A Leo must keep track of finances and room for storing items. They should ask, "Do I really love this piece, or am I buying it for the rush of acquiring something new?" A mindful approach prevents clutter or debt from overshadowing the pleasure of the hobby.

Scientific and Analytical Interests

A Drive for Invention
Though many see Leos as artistic, some are also drawn to science or technology. They might develop a skill for coding, engineering solutions, or researching space. Their creativity can help them approach problems differently. A Leo engineer might come up with fresh designs, while a Leo scientist might present findings with passion that influences others.

Leading Research Teams
If they work in a lab or project group, the leadership trait can shine.

A Leo might unify the team, boosting morale when setbacks happen. However, they must remain open to data-driven decisions rather than just personal hunches. The best labs function with collaboration and respect for details, so a balanced Leo can excel in guiding such environments.

Sharing Knowledge Publicly
Those who combine science with communication might write articles, speak at conferences, or create educational videos. They make dense information accessible through lively talks. Viewers or readers can catch the Leo's enthusiasm, possibly diving into the topic themselves. The challenge here is ensuring the content stays factual and accurate, even if the Leo loves dramatic presentation.

Balancing Multiple Hobbies

Tendency to Overcommit
Leos often find many interests appealing—performing, painting, sports, organizing, etc. The risk is taking on too much at once. They might sign up for a theater group, a debate club, and plan a fundraiser simultaneously, only to realize they do not have enough hours in the day. Stress or half-finished tasks might follow.

Time Management
Learning to prioritize helps them avoid feeling stretched thin. They can decide which hobbies matter most now and which can wait. By focusing on a few areas, they deepen their skills and get real satisfaction. They might schedule time blocks—like Tuesday evenings for art, weekends for volunteering—so each activity gets full attention.

Accepting Seasons of Focus
A wise Leo understands that life moves in phases. Maybe they spend one year honing painting techniques, then shift to event planning the next. Letting go of certain hobbies temporarily does not mean

failing; it simply recognizes that passion can flow in cycles. This approach can help them keep joy in each hobby instead of feeling forced to do everything at once.

Turning Hobbies into Careers

Professional Paths
Some Leos turn a favorite pursuit into a job—like an actor auditioning for bigger roles, an event organizer starting a business, or a graphic designer selling art. This can be exciting but also comes with real-world demands: marketing, customer service, financial records, and so on. If they fail to handle these, the hobby-turned-career could become stressful.

Balancing Passion and Practicality
Leos often thrive on passion, but a stable career also needs planning. If a Leo wants to open an art studio, they must research location, startup costs, potential clients, and competition. This step may feel less fun than creating art, but it is crucial. Once the business framework is set, they can shine in the creative aspect.

Staying Grounded
Even with a successful career in a beloved field, a Leo might face exhaustion if they blur all lines between work and personal life. For instance, if they sing at events for a living, they may lose the simple joy of singing at home for fun. Setting boundaries—like keeping certain hours for rest—helps maintain the love for the craft.

Friends and Group Activities

Shared Projects
Leos might gather friends for group hobbies, such as filming a short movie, putting on a talent show, or forming a local sports team. They excel at being the motivator, inspiring everyone to stay committed.

Group activities let them combine leadership with social bonding, building memories and forging closer ties.

Understanding Others' Roles
In group settings, a Leo should remember that not everyone wants to lead or be in the spotlight. Some prefer behind-the-scenes work or a quieter approach. Valuing each member's contribution—and not calling all the shots—keeps morale high. When a Leo recognizes what each friend brings to the table, the entire group benefits.

Rotating Leadership
To maintain harmony, sometimes the Leo can suggest rotating leadership: "This week, you make the plan, next week I'll do it." Letting someone else direct can be refreshing for the group and help the Leo see new methods of organizing. It also teaches them that stepping back does not reduce their importance; it often increases respect.

Personal Growth Through Hobbies

Confidence and Skill-Building
Engaging in hobbies can boost a Leo's self-esteem in healthy ways. As they see progress—improved acting, better cooking, faster running—they gain confidence based on real achievements. This is more stable than confidence that comes only from compliments.

Stress Relief
Hobbies offer a chance to unwind from daily pressures. A Leo might release tension by painting swirls of color or dribbling a soccer ball around the park. If they can set aside the desire to impress and simply enjoy the activity, they can find calm and renewal.

Discovering New Sides of Themselves
Trying different hobbies can reveal hidden talents or passions. A Leo might discover a love for pottery they never knew they had, or

realize they are great at teaching kids to swim. Exploring these avenues can spark growth and even open career doors. Plus, it shows them they are not limited to what they already know.

Pitfalls of Seeking Constant Admiration

Overusing Hobbies for Attention

It is natural for a Leo to enjoy applause. But if they pick hobbies mainly for praise, they might lose genuine satisfaction over time. They may drop an activity if the applause wanes, never seeing it through. For example, if a Leo learns guitar to get likes on social media but quits when views drop, they miss the deeper fun of music.

Comparisons and Jealousy

When a Leo sees someone else getting more recognition in the same hobby—say, a friend's YouTube channel grows faster—they might feel envious. They could push themselves to extremes or talk negatively about the other person. Recognizing that everyone's path is unique can lessen this jealousy. It helps to focus on personal improvement and the joy of the hobby itself.

Ignoring Personal Limits

A Leo who wants to excel might over-train in sports, risk injury, or stay up all night editing videos. Over time, burnout can happen. Balancing ambition with rest is essential. People often produce their best work when they feel recharged and enthusiastic, not when they are exhausted or pressured.

Encouraging a Leo's Hobbies

If you are a friend or family member, you can support a Leo's hobbies by:

Showing Genuine Interest: Ask them how a project is going, watch a performance, or look at their latest art.

Offering Honest Feedback: Praise is nice, but sincere critique helps them grow. If something can improve, gently mention it.

Providing Resources: If you know a helpful coach, share the info. If you see a contest for their skill, tell them about it.

Setting Joint Goals: Join them in the hobby if you have interest. Work together on a shared target—like finishing a painting series or training for a charity race.

The Joy of Continuous Learning

Never Done Growing

A remarkable trait of Leo is their adaptability when they truly set their mind to learning. Whether it is mastering a new cooking style, practicing a foreign language, or building furniture, they can apply their energy to keep advancing. This helps them stay curious through all stages of life.

Switching Hobbies Over Time

Leos might start with sports as teens, shift to photography in their 20s, pick up event planning in their 30s, and discover gardening in their 40s or beyond. Each phase can reflect changing priorities—like a calmer hobby when they want to unwind or a more social one when they crave group fun. It is all part of staying in tune with personal growth.

Finding Fulfillment

Ultimately, hobbies and skills can give a Leo more than external praise. They can foster new friendships, relieve stress, develop discipline, and reveal hidden gifts. A balanced Leo sees these activities as a means of expression and development, not just a path to show off. By treating each pursuit with respect and humility, they find deeper satisfaction than instant applause can offer.

CHAPTER 19: COMMON MISUNDERSTANDINGS ABOUT LEO

Leos are often described as bold and full of energy. Yet, along with these qualities come certain stereotypes or unclear ideas that can lead people to misunderstand them. From assuming that Leos must always be in charge to believing that they are all the same, these misconceptions can affect how Leos are treated—or even how they see themselves. In this chapter, we will explore the most frequent misunderstandings about Leos, explain where these ideas come from, and show the more realistic view. By the end, you will see that being a Leo does not mean fitting neatly into a single mold, but rather having a range of possibilities shaped by both personality and life experience.

"Leos Are Always Arrogant"

The Misconception:
One widespread belief is that Leos are constantly self-centered, always trying to show off how great they are. People might think of them as never listening to others and always bragging.

The Reality:
While it is true that some Leos enjoy being noticed, arrogance is not a built-in trait for all. Many Leos simply carry a natural confidence that others can see as proud. But healthy pride is different from being rude or dismissive. Confident Leos often encourage others to shine as well, welcoming group ideas and working together. They

can be quite supportive and caring, rather than dismissing everyone else. Problems arise only if a Leo focuses so much on the spotlight that they forget to share with others. But that is a choice, not a guarantee.

How This Misunderstanding Forms:
The lion symbol, plus the boldness many Leos display, can appear as if they value themselves too highly. Stories of a very showy or overly proud Leo can overshadow the many quieter or kinder examples.

"Leos Cannot Handle Criticism"

The Misconception:
Another myth says Leos lose their temper at any hint of critique and cannot see their own flaws. People assume that if you say anything negative to a Leo, they will explode.

The Reality:
Leos, like anyone, can be sensitive if feedback feels harsh or mocking. They do place importance on respect, so if a comment is insulting, they might respond strongly. Yet, many Leos do learn to handle useful suggestions calmly. If feedback is given politely—focusing on the issue rather than insulting them personally—chances are good that a Leo will listen, especially if they see a chance to improve. Many Leos appreciate genuine advice that helps them succeed, as long as it is not delivered in a humiliating way.

Why This Stereotype Persists:
When a Leo does react badly, it might be noticeable because they are not shy about showing emotion. Observers remember such dramatic episodes, forgetting the times a Leo accepted feedback calmly.

"All Leos Love the Spotlight 24/7"

The Misconception:
A strong cliché is that every Leo wants the stage every minute—never content unless they are the center of attention.

The Reality:
While Leos often enjoy sharing talents or leading, many also value calm moments. Some are more introverted, expressing their traits through writing, art, or private accomplishments. They may still have that inner sense of dignity and self-worth but do not necessarily want an audience for all they do. Even the more outgoing Leos need periods of rest or quiet reflection. They can find too much constant attention tiring.

Roots of the Misunderstanding:
The lion symbol and stories of extremely extroverted Leos overshadow the reality that a range of social comfort levels exist in this sign. Those who do love a stage might be highly visible, shaping public opinion of the sign.

"Leos Never Get Hurt or Upset"

The Misconception:
Because of their bright energy, some think Leos never feel sad or worried. They seem so positive that people imagine they are always brave and unaffected.

The Reality:
Leos can feel emotions very deeply. Their sunny exterior can hide insecurities or sorrow. A Leo might worry about losing approval, failing to meet goals, or not living up to personal ideals. They can get upset if they sense betrayal, feel unappreciated, or face any problem that harms their sense of self. Like anyone, they need understanding when they are hurt. The difference is that some Leos may mask

these feelings to appear strong, leading others to think they are just fine.

Why This Idea Lasts:
A confident presence can make it look like nothing touches them. But underneath that pride can be a sensitive heart that longs for acceptance and understanding.

"Leos Demand Control in All Situations"

The Misconception:
There is a popular image of Leos being tyrannical in groups—always barking orders and refusing to listen.

The Reality:
Yes, many Leos enjoy leadership, but good leadership is not about giving commands nonstop. A wise Leo seeks to inspire, organize, and solve problems with the team. Plenty of Leos are happy to follow if someone else's plan is strong or if the group is already well-led. They just do not shy away from stepping up if they see confusion and think they can help. They might speak out more readily than quieter personalities, yet that does not mean they refuse to collaborate or follow a capable leader.

Contributing Factors:
If a Leo only sees poor organization, they could feel forced to take charge. But if roles are clearly set and the group runs smoothly, a Leo might enjoy being a supportive member. The public only notices the forceful side when a Leo faces disorder or tries to fix issues.

"Leos Are Only About Themselves"

The Misconception:
Some believe Leos never show empathy or interest in others,

picturing them as self-absorbed people who ignore everyone else's needs.

The Reality:
Leos can be incredibly protective and generous. They might go out of their way to help a struggling friend or relative, using their natural warmth to comfort and motivate. If a Leo sees someone being mistreated, they may speak up. Their strong self-awareness does not automatically mean they lack empathy. When they care about someone, they care with intensity, giving both emotional support and practical assistance.

Why It Happens:
Moments when a Leo focuses on personal ambitions or displays big confidence can appear self-centered. However, focusing on personal growth does not cancel out the ability to care for others. The two can coexist if the Leo balances personal goals with generosity.

"Leos Always Need to Be Loud and Flashy"

The Misconception:
Another myth is that every Leo must wear bold outfits, talk in a booming voice, and dominate social media with dramatic posts.

The Reality:
While some Leos dress in bright colors or speak with flair, others might have a subtle style, showing their uniqueness through small details or thoughtful statements. They might prefer quiet elegance over flashiness. The sign's link to boldness can manifest internally, as a steady sense of self, rather than in outward flamboyance. Also, cultural background, upbringing, and personal taste shape whether a Leo's style is minimal or extravagant.

Where the Image Comes From:
Stories or examples of extremely showy Leos often stand out in

memory. This leads to the false impression that all must behave that way. In reality, personality is influenced by many factors, not just zodiac sign.

"Leos Do Not Follow Rules or Take Orders"

The Misconception:
Because Leos are known for leadership, some assume they cannot function in settings with clear rules or directions, believing they must always break the mold.

The Reality:
Plenty of Leos excel in structured environments—like corporate offices, the military, or other places with a chain of command. They can respect authority if they believe in the larger mission or see that the leaders are competent. If the system is fair, a Leo might adapt quite well, bringing enthusiasm and creative problem-solving. Only when they face disorganized or unjust leadership do they push back strongly.

Why People Think This:
The sign's independent vibe can be misread. Yes, a Leo may question rules that feel pointless. But they are not necessarily rebellious just for the sake of it. They want respect and logic in any hierarchy.

"All Leos Are the Same"

The Misconception:
Some stereotypes paint every Leo with one brush—loud, flashy, bossy, and so on—implying zero variation.

The Reality:
Astrology can suggest broad themes, but each person's life story, environment, and choices shape how they express these themes. A

shy Leo may show confidence in private ways—like quietly standing firm in beliefs, or creating art that speaks for them. Another might be an extrovert, organizing large community events. Even those who share the lion sign can differ in humor, daily habits, or personal dreams. Some might be modest in style, others flamboyant. Personality is layered, not set by a single label.

Why It Persists:
Simple zodiac stereotypes can be catchy: "Leo equals loud." But real individuals are more complex. Observing several Leos reveals how diverse they can be, from calm teachers to energetic entertainers.

"Leos Do Not Value Teamwork"

The Misconception:
People may claim that Leos never cooperate, always wanting to be in charge and ignoring group cohesion.

The Reality:
A well-balanced Leo often thrives in teams, especially when they see the overall goal as meaningful. They can bring cheer, organization, and motivation. It is true that if no one takes the lead, a Leo might step forward. But that does not cancel the ability to listen to ideas or share successes. They can be quite friendly colleagues, celebrating others' efforts and championing group members. What they dislike is a vague team with no direction, which can spark them to push for structure.

Why the Myth Spread:
A Leo's willingness to speak up can be mislabeled as ignoring others. But in many cases, the Leo is simply trying to help the group move forward. If the team dynamic is healthy, Leos do not sabotage it—they enhance it.

"Leos Only Want Success and Fame"

The Misconception:
Critics sometimes say Leos care about personal gain—money, fancy titles, or being recognized everywhere—more than anything else.

The Reality:
Leos do appreciate recognition, but not all are chasing big fame. Many simply want respect in their field or from their community. They might be happy as a teacher who encourages students, a craftsman quietly perfecting a skill, or a volunteer organizer making a local difference. For them, "success" might mean helping others, running a stable household, or excelling in a quiet hobby. Fame or fortune is not always the end goal—feeling proud of their contributions often matters more.

Reason for the Myth:
Some famous figures are indeed Leos who love the limelight. People notice those high-profile examples and assume every Leo must want the same. Meanwhile, countless lesser-known Leos lead fulfilling lives without chasing stardom.

"Leos Are Always Dramatic and Emotional"

The Misconception:
Because of their strong presence, people think Leos always exaggerate, blow up small issues, or have huge emotional reactions.

The Reality:
Yes, some Leos express emotions vividly, but "always" is too broad. Many can stay calm and composed, only showing drama in specific moments—such as celebrating a friend's success or confronting a real injustice. Others might channel feeling through creative work rather than emotional outbursts. So, while a lion might roar

sometimes, they also know how to be peaceful. It depends on the situation and the individual's temperament.

Why People Believe It:
We tend to recall events where a Leo made a scene, ignoring all the normal, calm interactions. Over time, those memorable stories feed a stereotype that "Leos are always dramatic."

"Leos Cannot Be Introverted"

The Misconception:
There is a perception that every Leo must be outgoing, loud, and social—never shy or introspective.

The Reality:
Introverted Leos exist. They may still have a strong sense of self but choose to speak only when needed, or prefer smaller groups over big parties. They might reflect carefully before talking, or express themselves through art or writing. A quiet Leo can be just as proud and confident internally, but not show it through big gestures. They might gently stand their ground in private ways. The sign's typical traits—like leadership or self-assurance—do not have to appear as extroversion.

How the Myth Grew:
Many mainstream horoscope sources feature the "roaring lion" image. People rarely highlight an introverted Leo who leads behind the scenes or fosters deep connections one-on-one. But such individuals are out there.

"A Leo's Creativity Only Involves Performance"

The Misconception:
Some assume all creative Leos are actors, dancers, or singers, leaving out other forms of creativity.

The Reality:
Creativity can show up in technology, design, writing, culinary arts, or even problem-solving in business. A Leo might excel at coding innovative software, crafting unique recipes, or planning unusual event themes. The imagination typical of the sign often merges with a desire to share or shape experiences, but it does not have to be limited to performing arts. Some Leos might pour creativity into their personal style or home décor, quietly letting that energy shine in everyday surroundings.

Why It Occurs:
Stereotypes linking Leos to theatrical pursuits overshadow quieter, more subtle forms of creativity. People forget that behind many well-run organizations or well-crafted products might stand a Leo applying creative thinking.

"All Leos Are Party Animals"

The Misconception:
Because some Leos enjoy lively social scenes, partying, or hosting big gatherings, others think every Leo constantly goes out, loves loud music, and runs from one event to another.

The Reality:
Party-loving Leos do exist, but others find peace in smaller get-togethers or even quiet nights reading or watching a movie. Social style can vary widely: a Leo teacher might prefer dinner with a few friends to share deep chats, or a Leo entrepreneur might mix business socials with calm weekends at home. Even those who do like parties often need times to rest or do personal hobbies. The sign does not always mean constant partying.

Reason for This Stereotype:
Again, flashy stories stand out. A single night of a Leo dancing at the center of a party could paint an inaccurate picture that they do this

every day. People seldom pay equal attention to a quiet evening the same Leo enjoys at home.

"Leos Never Feel Fearful or Unsure"

The Misconception:
A big myth is that Leos are immune to fear, unstoppable in every circumstance.

The Reality:
No one is above feeling fear or uncertainty sometimes. Leos might be brave in certain areas—like public speaking—but can be uneasy in others, such as making major financial decisions or showing deep vulnerability in a relationship. When they do feel uncertain, a Leo may hide it behind a confident stance, hoping to solve the problem alone. However, if they find supportive friends or mentors, they can admit their worries and realize it is okay to not always feel bold.

Where It Comes From:
People see a Leo's strong front and assume it is real in every situation. They do not realize that behind that calm face, a Leo could be carefully weighing risks or quietly dealing with nerves.

"Leos Must Have Expensive Tastes"

The Misconception:
Because of the sign's link to grandeur, there is a belief that all Leos need luxury brands, fancy decorations, and top-of-the-line gadgets.

The Reality:
While some Leos do favor high-quality or stylish items, "expensive" is not always the goal. They might choose bright colors or unique designs that suit their taste, not necessarily the highest price tag. Many Leos can be practical with money, looking for deals or supporting local crafts instead of big brands. They often aim for

items that reflect their personality, which might be something custom-made or handmade, not necessarily the most costly. Liking beauty or flair does not always mean being lavish.

Why the Myth Sticks:
Stories of a glamorous Leo spending a lot of money stay in people's minds, creating the image that all Leos are extravagant. In truth, personal values and the situation can shape how a Leo spends or saves.

"Leos Only Care About Appearance"

The Misconception:
Tied to luxury myths is the notion that Leos are shallow, focusing on looks—either their own or others'—and ignoring deeper qualities.

The Reality:
Though many Leos appreciate looking put-together and may notice style, they also value loyalty, kindness, and intelligence. They might dress carefully to feel confident, but do not automatically dismiss someone because of simple clothes. Friendships or partnerships for a Leo often rely on emotional connection, shared values, or good humor. If someone stands for honesty and is supportive, a Leo can be drawn to them, no matter how they dress.

Where It Arises:
When you see a Leo obviously proud of a new outfit or complimenting someone's style, you might think they care only about appearances. In reality, they can also admire someone's warmth, creativity, or strength. Looks are just one piece of the puzzle.

"Leos Are Always in a Good Mood"

The Misconception:
Since Leos are connected with bright energy and the sun, some people think they are always cheerful, the life of every gathering, never down or serious.

The Reality:
Leos do bring positivity at times, but they also experience stress, sadness, or anger. It might be that they choose to present a smile or a "can-do" attitude, trying to keep others' spirits up. But that does not mean they feel that way constantly on the inside. If something serious happens, they might temporarily lose that sunshine. They just usually bounce back with optimistic thinking or direct action once they process the problem.

Why People Think This:
Seeing a Leo being the fun host or encouraging a friend, one might assume they are always that uplifting. But everyone has moments of exhaustion or frustration. A Leo can hide those moments if they think the group depends on their positive energy. Only close friends might see when they are not feeling bright.

Embracing the Real Leo

Moving Past Misconceptions
These misunderstandings are common because of strong stereotypes. When you meet a Leo who behaves differently—maybe a shy one, a calm listener, or someone who handles criticism well—it can be surprising if you only know the "big roar" legend. However, keeping an open mind lets you see that each Leo is an individual with unique strengths, quirks, and growth areas.

How to Foster Better Understanding
If you are a Leo, you might sometimes feel confined by these

sweeping assumptions. Stay true to who you are—recognize that you do not have to fit a script. If others expect you to be loud or controlling, you can politely show them another side. If you love the spotlight, that is fine, but you are not obligated to seek it every day. Communication—telling people how you truly feel—often clears up confusion.

If you are someone who knows a Leo, ask questions and observe them as a person, not just as a sign. Notice how they react to different scenarios, what truly excites them, and how they choose to solve problems. By doing so, you will likely see the lion's heart in a deeper, more genuine way.

Realizing the Range

Ultimately, the sign of Leo covers a wide spectrum. Confident or quiet, creative or methodical, every Leo combines personal life experiences with typical lion-like passion. Myths vanish as we see that, yes, they can be dynamic leaders or performers, but they can also be thoughtful, introverted, caring, or humble. By breaking down misunderstandings, we free Leos—and the people around them—to have richer, truer connections.

CHAPTER 20: INTERESTING FACTS ABOUT LEO

Leos have captured people's imaginations for centuries, spurring myths, stories, and modern discussions about what this sign means. Beyond the common traits of leadership and creativity, there are numerous lesser-known tidbits that can shed light on why Leos are so captivating. In this final chapter, we will look at some interesting facts related to Leo—from its constellation origins to modern research findings that might surprise you. We will also explore how Leos appear in various cultures and contexts, highlighting the diverse ways people interpret this fiery sign.

The Constellation in Ancient Times

Origins in the Stars
Leo is one of the earliest recognized constellations. Ancient stargazers in Mesopotamia, Greece, and other places noticed a grouping of stars they thought looked like a lion. These stories took root in mythology, linking the lion shape to tales of heroism or royalty. Over time, the constellation's presence in the sky around mid-summer (in the Northern Hemisphere) gave it a link to warmth and brightness.

Nemean Lion Myth
One well-known Greek myth is the tale of the Nemean Lion, a nearly invincible beast defeated by the hero Hercules. Afterward, the lion was placed among the stars as the Leo constellation to mark the feat. This story adds a heroic, mythical dimension, suggesting Leo's connection to courage and a brave heart.

Regulus, the Royal Star

Within the Leo constellation sits Regulus—often called the "kingly star." Bright and near the "heart" of the lion, it was historically viewed as a symbol of rulership. Astrologers sometimes see it as embodying noble energy, aligning well with the typical image of a confident, proud sign.

Leo's Link to the Sun

Ruled by the Sun

Astrologically, each sign is said to have a ruling planet or luminary, and for Leo, that is the Sun. The Sun is the center of our solar system, shining light and warmth on Earth. This is often why Leos are connected with brightness, generosity, and the idea of "shining." They may carry a sunny disposition or a wish to share positivity with others.

Solar Symbolism

In various traditions, the Sun represents vitality, creativity, and life force. These attributes match well with the typical Leo nature: life-affirming, outgoing, and warm. However, just like the Sun can burn if you stand in it for too long, a Leo's intensity might feel overwhelming if not balanced. This solar connection underscores both the sign's radiant potential and the importance of managing that energy kindly.

A Summery Sign

In many places, Leo season (late July to late August) falls in the midst of summer's heat (in the Northern Hemisphere). This time of year often brings social gatherings, vacations, and a sense of fun. Thus, the sign of Leo is often associated with spirited social energy, mirroring summertime festivities in these regions.

Cultural Appearances of Leo Symbolism

Egyptian Imagery
In ancient Egypt, lions were sometimes linked with royalty and guardianship. Statues like the Sphinx, though featuring a human head, carry a lion's body. This lion form represented power and watchfulness. Such themes echo the protective side of Leos in modern astrology—though these Egyptian figures were not strictly about zodiac signs, the ideas overlap in how lions represent strength and guardianship.

Chinese Astrology
Chinese astrology is entirely different from the Western zodiac, based on a 12-year cycle of animal signs rather than star constellations. However, some playful comparisons occur. While there is no "lion" sign in the Chinese zodiac, a person with the Western sign of Leo might look for parallels in the Tiger or Dragon signs for certain traits like bravery or a commanding spirit. These cross-cultural musings are not official but show how societies link large, bold creatures with leadership qualities.

Art and Heraldry
Lions commonly appear in European heraldry—coats of arms, flags, and royal symbols. For centuries, a lion image was used to mark bravery or a regal family line. Though not tied directly to astrology, it shows how strongly the lion shape resonates as a sign of honor, protection, and sometimes fierce determination. These global uses of lion imagery align with key Leo themes but exist independently of the zodiac.

Modern Research on Zodiac Birth Patterns

Season of Birth Effects
Some modern studies explore how birth months might affect

traits—though they do not usually attribute this to astrology in a formal sense. For instance, certain research looks at how daylight exposure or seasonal factors might shape mood or health. If a child is born in late summer, they might have different early experiences than one born in winter. Whether that leads to the typical "Leo personality" is debated. Still, it is an interesting angle: environmental influences in the first months of life might subtly shape temperament or physical development.

Popularity of Leo Birthdays

Because late July to mid-August is a break period for many schools in the Northern Hemisphere, some parents note that Leo children might celebrate birthdays differently—perhaps with more outdoor parties or summer-themed events. This could, in theory, feed into a confident social vibe if they frequently gather friends for big celebrations. Of course, this is not a scientific rule but a fun observation about how environment and timing can coincide.

Celebrity Leos and Public Figures

Actors and Performers

The entertainment industry has seen many prominent Leos who love performing. Famous examples often show strong on-screen presence or a flair for stage performance. These stories feed the idea that Leos excel where creativity meets public attention.

Leaders and Innovators

Leos also appear among influential leaders, from business founders to political trailblazers. They might bring bold visions, rallying teams around new ideas. This pattern is not proof that every Leo leads with brilliance, but it demonstrates how certain traits—confidence, drive, warmth—can help them stand out in leadership arenas.

Recognizing Variety

However, plenty of Leos are not global superstars or top executives.

They thrive in everyday roles—maybe as an inspiring teacher, a cheerful customer service rep, or a dedicated nurse. Their "star quality" might show up in smaller circles but still be felt by those they serve or interact with. We often just hear about the big names, forgetting the quiet yet meaningful roles a Leo can fill.

Symbols and Colors Linked to Leo

Traditional Color Associations
Gold, orange, yellow, and sometimes red are often tied to Leo. These colors evoke the Sun, warmth, and a fiery spirit. Many Leos resonate with these shades, though not all feel compelled to wear them. The idea is that these hues match the energetic or "glowing" essence commonly associated with the sign.

Leo Element: Fire
In Western astrology, Leo is part of the fire element group, along with Aries and Sagittarius. Fire signs are said to represent enthusiasm, action, and a sense of passion. This can be seen in how some Leos approach challenges—by charging forward, possibly with dramatic flair. Fire's qualities remind us that Leo's energy can warm and inspire but can also scorch if taken too far.

Leo's Metal and Gemstone
Sometimes, traditions mention gold as Leo's metal, again linked to the Sun and bright shine. In gemstones, the ruby or peridot is sometimes named as a Leo stone, said to enhance qualities like courage or positivity. Of course, these symbolic links vary among different sources, but they reinforce the idea of brightness and value.

Leo Connections in Literature

Famous Characters
Authors have created memorable characters who reflect Leo-like

traits: brave, proud, or protective. Sometimes these are literal lions, other times humans who symbolize leonine qualities—like a bold king or queen, or a fearless adventurer. These characters often help readers grasp the emotional depth and power that a lion archetype can carry.

Themes of Courage and Heart

Stories referencing a lion's heart often highlight unwavering loyalty, sense of honor, and the willingness to defend what is right. Even in fantasy tales, a lion might represent hope or the rightful ruler. While these references are not always about astrology, they show that across cultures, the lion stands for certain enduring ideals that resonate with traits often linked to Leo.

Unusual Facts about the Leo Constellation

Shifting Position

Because of Earth's axial precession over thousands of years, the precise alignment of the Sun with the Leo constellation changes slowly. Some modern astronomy sources note that during a given year, the Sun might appear in front of different constellations than the traditional zodiac times indicate. Still, astrology usually keeps the set zodiac date ranges.

Denebola and Other Stars

Denebola is another star in Leo, marking the "tail" of the lion shape. While Regulus is the most famous star, others like Denebola, Algieba, and Zosma add to the constellation's distinct pattern. Stargazers who want to identify Leo can learn to spot the backward question mark (commonly called the Sickle) that forms the lion's mane and shoulders.

Meteor Showers

The Leonids meteor shower, peaking around mid-November, seems to radiate from the Leo constellation area. Every year, watchers can see shooting stars from these dust trails left by a comet. This link to "falling stars" can enchant fans of both astronomy and astrology, though it is purely a celestial phenomenon not directly tied to personality traits.

Modern Pop Culture Influences

Online Memes and Buzz
Leos often star in social media jokes or memes, highlighting themes like "the one who insists on being the main character." While humorous, these can cement stereotypes if repeated without nuance. Some Leos embrace the humor and respond with playful pride; others find it oversimplifies who they are.

Fashion and Marketing
Because of the sign's strong brand-like identity, some companies use lion imagery or "Leo-like" slogans to market items in August. You might see clothing lines or promotional campaigns referencing the lion's fierce or bright vibe. This can be fun for consumers who identify with the sign, though it is mostly a marketing strategy rather than deep astrological meaning.

Music and Art References
Some musicians create songs referencing the lion or the sun, symbolizing strength or personal empowerment. Artists might incorporate lion motifs to suggest boldness or courage. These creative references keep the lion symbol fresh in modern pop culture, linking it to ongoing ideas of valor, self-belief, and warmth.

Studies on Personality Patterns

Psychology vs. Astrology
Strictly scientific psychology does not typically support the notion that zodiac signs alone determine personality. However, people sometimes notice patterns that match their birth chart.

Confirmation bias might play a role, where we observe details that confirm our beliefs about zodiac traits. Still, many folks find astrology helpful as a tool for self-reflection, not as an unchangeable rulebook.

Common Threads

Even without strict evidence, we see in practice that many Leos do show strong creativity, leadership, or loyalty. Is it purely coincidence, or shaped by cultural prompts (like hearing about Leo traits and choosing to live up to them)? The debate continues. Regardless, noticing these patterns can inspire personal growth—for instance, a Leo might aim to lead responsibly because they resonate with the idea of being a mindful leader.

Surprising Leo Hobbies

Calming Interests

We often associate Leos with big, loud pursuits, but some genuinely love peaceful hobbies like gardening, birdwatching, or pottery. The sign's bold energy can also channel into nurturing or fine detail tasks. For them, it might be a peaceful break from the demands of daily life.

Analytical Projects

Some Leos enjoy research or puzzle-solving, investigating deeply into topics that fascinate them—like collecting data on local wildlife or tinkering with mechanical devices. This methodical approach can surprise people who assume all Leos are showy. Yet, the same determination can drive them to master these quieter interests.

Leos and Their Furry Counterparts

The Real Animal

Real lions in the wild reflect both regal group bonding (living in prides) and fierce protection. Some parallel that to how Leos cherish their "pride" of friends and family, showing loyalty and readiness to defend. That said, real lions behave according to natural instincts. Linking them fully to human personalities is just symbolic fun.

Animal Symbolism

Beyond the simple notion of "lion equals bravery," some traditions link lions to generosity—feeding and protecting the pride's cubs. Others see the lion's roar as a call for recognition. Humans with Leo traits might identify with these images, picking the aspects that resonate with them personally.

Self-Reflection and Leo Energy

Seasonal Check-Ins

During the time of year called "Leo season," some people reflect on how they can be more open-hearted, more creative, or more confident. Even those who do not strongly follow astrology may enjoy a sense of summer renewal, setting fresh goals or reconnecting with friends. For Leos, it might be a natural time to assess achievements since their last birthday.

Embracing or Tweaking Traits

A person with strong Leo influences might reflect: "Am I overdoing my need for praise? Could I share leadership more?" Or, "How can I put my talents to better use?" These questions help them shape their growth, aligning that signature lion energy with mindful choices. Real power often lies in harnessing one's best qualities while moderating the extremes.

Notable Leo Strengths

Generosity: Leos often give time or resources, whether hosting events or supporting a cause.

Protectiveness: Like lions guarding their cubs, they stand up for loved ones or those treated unfairly.

Optimism: Many keep morale high, believing solutions are possible. This can motivate groups during tough times.

Drive to Create: Their mind brims with ideas for art, projects, or ways to make life more colorful.

Loyalty: They can be steadfast friends, standing by those they trust through ups and downs.

Leos and Personal Goals

Pursuing Big Targets

Because Leos often think in big terms, they might set lofty objectives—opening a business, writing a novel, running a marathon. This can inspire them to work hard, surprising skeptics who only see them as wanting attention. If they focus, a Leo can turn that bright imagination into real achievements.

Self-Improvement Focus

Leos might set personal growth goals, like improving communication skills or learning to handle conflict calmly. They do not only want external success; many also want to be known as good friends, helpful leaders, or caring partners. That combination of external drive and internal betterment can help them stay balanced.

Worldwide Observances

Zodiac-Themed Merchandise

In some countries, shops highlight zodiac-based items—like Leo T-shirts, lion jewelry, or stationery with fiery designs—especially around late July through August. People might exchange small items with a lion symbol to mark a Leo's birthday. This commercial side can be playful, but it also shows how deeply the sign is woven into everyday culture.

Astro-Festivals
Some communities hold informal events that look at star lore, including Leo's constellation, or that gather individuals from each zodiac sign. While not official festivals, they create a place to learn about star myths. Leos might host or speak at such events, using their natural gift for entertaining or explaining stories about the stars.

Interaction with Other Fire Signs

Aries and Sagittarius
In typical Western astrology, Aries, Leo, and Sagittarius are the three fire signs, each with its own style of boldness. Aries is quick and direct, Leo is proud and warm, while Sagittarius is adventurous and philosophical. They often vibe well together, sparking lively debates or creative collaborations. However, their combined energies can also lead to conflicts if no one compromises. They might all want to set the direction.

Differing Flames
A deeper look reveals that each fire sign expresses that element differently. Leo focuses on consistent warmth and the desire to nurture big visions, Aries on initiating action, and Sagittarius on exploring broad ideas or beliefs. Recognizing these nuances helps them respect each other's approach.

Leo in Family and Friend Circles

Central Bonds
In a family, the Leo might become a unifying presence, bringing folks together for gatherings or bridging misunderstandings with positivity. They might be the one who organizes a special meal or an

outing, wanting everyone to bond. Friends might rely on a Leo to cheer them up or plan fun activities.

Caution with Overcommitment

Because of their big heart, a Leo may promise too much—like helping every friend move or hosting many events. Balancing the urge to assist with their own well-being is key. Loved ones can gently remind them to take breaks, so they do not run themselves ragged.

Scientific Curiosity About Astrology

Lack of Scientific Proof

It is worth noting that mainstream science does not confirm that zodiac signs cause personality traits. The positions of the stars, as we see them, do not show a proven link to how someone behaves. People born under different signs may share or differ in traits for many reasons—culture, upbringing, genetics, personal choice.

Personal and Cultural Value

Even so, many find astrology interesting as a lens for self-reflection, conversation, or creative thinking about life patterns. Leo's popularity remains because the lion archetype resonates emotionally with ideas of courage, affection, and personal shining. Whether someone believes strongly in astrology or sees it as a fun theme, the sign of Leo has become a symbol of certain ideals.

Last Thoughts on Leo's Vibrant Tapestry

Leo stands as a sign that has fascinated people from ancient times to the modern day. From myths of the Nemean Lion to the intense brightness of the midday sun, the symbolism captures hearts. While we often see Leos as bold leaders or radiant performers, they also harbor quiet strength, varied interests, and a caring spirit. These interesting facts—spanning astronomy, cultural references, modern findings, and daily life—remind us that there is far more to Leo than the usual stereotypes.

In the end, understanding these details can help Leos appreciate their own heritage and can guide others to see the sign with fresh eyes. Whether it is the constellation's storied past, the creative spark of a modern Leo, or the steadfast loyalty they offer friends, the lion's essence endures. By blending knowledge of classic astrology with today's perspectives, we see a sign that continues to evolve, shining as brightly as ever for those who look its way. And for the Leos themselves, these facts may serve as inspiration to keep sharing warmth with the world, in whatever paths they choose.

Help Us Share Your Thoughts!

Dear reader,

Thank you for spending your time with this book. We hope it brought you enjoyment and a few new ideas to think about. If there was anything that didn't work for you, or if you have suggestions on how we can improve, please let us know at **kontakt@skriuwer.com**. Your feedback means a lot to us and helps us make our books even better.

If you enjoyed this book, we would be very grateful if you left a review on the site where you purchased it. Your review not only helps other readers find our books, but also encourages us to keep creating more stories and materials that you'll love.

By choosing Skriuwer, you're also supporting **Frisian**—a minority language mainly spoken in the northern Netherlands. Although **Frisian** has a rich history, the number of speakers is shrinking, and it's at risk of dying out. Your purchase helps fund resources to preserve and promote this language, such as educational programs and learning tools. If you'd like to learn more about Frisian or even start learning it yourself, please visit **www.learnfrisian.com**.

Thank you for being part of our community. We look forward to sharing more books with you in the future.

Warm regards,
The Skriuwer Team

www.ingramcontent.com/pod-product-compliance
Lightning Source LLC
LaVergne TN
LVHW012039070526
838202LV00056B/5540